ADVERTISING

Winston Fletcher

Editorial Adviser
Ronald Chappell
Dean of the Faculty of Social Sciences,
Harrow College of Technology and Art

Drawings by
Jean Fletcher

TEACH YOURSELF BOOKS
Hodder and Stoughton

Fourth impression 1979

ISBN 0 340 222395

Printed and bound in Great Britain for Hodder and Stoughton Paperbacks, a Division of Hodder and Stoughton Ltd, Mill Road, Dunton Green, Sevenoaks, Kent (Editorial Office: 47 Bedford Square, London WC1 3DP) by Richard Clay (The Chaucer Press) Ltd, Bungay, Suffolk

Contents

Acknowledgements

I should like to express my grateful thanks to Eric McGregor, the author of the previous edition of *Teach Yourself Advertising* for suggesting that I write this new edition and for encouraging me to do so; to Norman Hart of the CAM Education Foundation for checking the chapter on how to get into advertising; to the Institute of Practitioners in Advertising and the Advertising Association for providing me with so much data; to Ken Dowley for vetting and improving the chapter on media; to John Harmer for likewise vetting and improving the section on production and to Jane Manwaring for so patiently typing and retyping my illegible manuscripts.

ADVERTISING

Winston Fletcher is Managing Director of the Fletcher Shelton advertising agency and has brought to this book his wide experience of modern trends and practice in advertising. The author of *The Admakers,* and a regular contributor to *Campaign* and *The Financial Times,* he also lectures frequently to groups both inside and outside the advertising world.

TEACH YOURSELF BOOKS

Introduction

How does advertising work? Why do companies spend so much on it? Is it really necessary? What are the techniques that advertisers' use? Who really benefits from advertising? Is it really honest? Could it be improved?

Advertising impinges upon all of our lives, hundreds and often thousands of times each day. In newspapers and magazines, on radio and television, in our post and on posters, on billboards and buses advertisements greet us, tempt us, inform us and amuse us. The importance of advertising in Western countries can be demonstrated by the volume of money spent on it: in Britain, advertising expenditure exceeds £1,000 million annually; in the U.S.A. the figure is $26,000 million; Germany and France spend about as much as Britain, Japan almost twice as much.

This new edition of *Teach Yourself Advertising* has been written both for students and, more generally, for readers throughout the world who wish to understand the background to this fascinating subject. While the ground it covers is essential knowledge for any advertising student, it contains a wealth of facts and case histories that will answer the questions that everyone, everywhere, asks about advertising from time to time.

Also *Teach Yourself Advertising* contains much new information that has never before been widely published outside the advertising industry itself. It includes data on how much advertising money is spent, where it is spent and who spends it—information previously not available in such comprehensive detail.

The plan of the book is to take the reader through the entire advertising business in the most straightforward and logical way. The first chapter defines advertising very precisely, and goes on briefly to trace how it has developed and grown to its position of major importance today.

The following three chapters describe the 3-way structure of the advertising business: the advertisers, who they are and how much they spend; the media in which the advertisements appear; and the advertising agencies which create the advertisements themselves. Chapter 5 shows how the whole process knits together from start to finish—how an advertising campaign is planned, produced and finally appears.

Chapter 6 looks at whether it all works and answers the question by revealing the modern research and testing techniques that advertisers use. Chapter 7 covers the vital subject of how advertising is controlled both in Britain and abroad, and also the relationship between advertising and consumerism. In Chapters 8 and 9 the roles of advertising internationally and in economic theory are studied, before finally Chapter 10 informs those wishing to work in advertising exactly how to go about getting a job.

A particular innovation in this book is the introduction of *Think Exercises* at the end of each of the first eight chapters. These Think Exercises are short, stimulating problem questions designed to tax your growing knowledge and understanding of advertising as the book progresses. The Think Exercises are intended to be enjoyable as well as educational; but for more serious students a selection of questions from recent examination papers set by the Communications, Advertising and Marketing Foundation are included in Appendix 2, and a full Bibliography is to be found in Appendix 3.

Advertising arouses more passionate controversy than almost any other industry, but few people really understand how and why it works. *Teach Yourself Advertising* has been written to answer the many questions about advertising that everybody asks.

The Faces of Advertising

People who work in advertising quickly become accustomed to the following snatch of recurrent conversation:

> 'What's your job?'
>
> 'I'm in advertising.'
>
> 'Oh, advertising! Do you do those Coca-Cola commercials on television? Or the Kelloggs? Or the Lux ones? I *hate* the Lux ones.'

When you work in advertising it is an irritating conversation. People outside invariably and thoughtlessly believe that a job in advertising consists mostly of making television commercials. Whereas in reality commercials on television are but a small part of the business—the very visible tip of the iceberg, the remaining nine-tenths of which most people are either unaware of or simply forget.

What is advertising?

What is advertising? It is a word in common usage, and we all think we know its meaning perfectly well. Yet like many other apparently simple words, the closer you look at it the more remarkably difficult it becomes to define precisely. The *Oxford Dictionary* offers five definitions of the verb *to advertise*, and four of the noun *advertisement*, of which the closest to modern usage is: 'a paid announcement in a newspaper'. Well *a paid announcement*, yes: and the word *paid* is, as we shall see, crucial to the definition. However, *in a newspaper* obviously will not do: advertisements can and do appear on television, radio, posters, matchboxes, train tickets, book jackets, in cinemas and shop windows and a hundred-and-one other places.

The best definition of 'advertisement' that I know was written by Jeremy Bullmore, Chairman of J. Walter Thompson in London:

> 'An advertisement is a paid-for communication intended to inform and/or influence one or more people.'

It is illuminating to examine this definition in detail. First: *'paid-for'*. As has already been pointed out, an 'advertisement' that is not paid for is not, in the strictly technical sense, an advertisement at all. Its cost may be minimal, as when a farmer paints a sign like 'FARM FRESH EGGS—TURN RIGHT'. But if literally no cost at all is involved then the communication may be publicity, may be persuasive, may be propaganda, but it is not technically *advertising*.

Secondly: *'communication'*. Every advertisement is attempting to bridge a gap between a sender and one or more

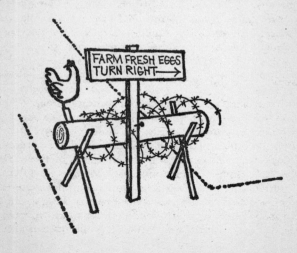

potential receivers. That bridge is a form of communication. To buy a whole page in a newspaper and leave it absolutely blank is not to advertise. There must, in other words, be message as well as medium.

Thirdly: '*intended*'. As we shall see, particularly in Chapter 6, not all advertisements 'work' in the sense of achieving their desired objectives. Most of us have, on one occasion or another, placed a 'For Sale' advertisement in the classified advertisements column of a newspaper. Often such an advertisement may achieve no effective response whatsoever. The fact that it has failed to achieve its intended objective does not detract from the fact that it is an advertisement. It is the intention that counts.

Fourthly: '*inform and/or influence*'. Many people, usually critics antagonistic to advertising, have sought to draw a distinction between *informative* and *persuasive* advertisements. In this context, *informative* advertisements are customarily thought to be acceptable and desirable; *persuasive* advertisements are thought to be less acceptable, or even totally unacceptable. In practice the line between informative and persuasive advertising is impossible to draw. All the *information* which an advertiser chooses to put into his advertisement is intended to be *persuasive*. But since the *persuasive* content advertising is sometimes deprecated—particularly in Communist countries, where the volume of advertising is rapidly growing (see Chapter 8)—it is perhaps less contentious to say that all advertisements necessarily aim to 'inform and/or influence'. An advertisement which aimed to have no influence whatsoever could hardly be an advertisement.

Finally: '*one or more people*'. All advertisements are addressed to people. Sometimes just to one person ('*Chuckles. Be my Valentine and I shall be yours eternally. M.*'), sometimes to many millions (*Guinness is Good for You*). Inevitably, to return to the opening of this chapter, people outside advertising think of consumer goods advertisements addressed to mass audiences as being What Advertising Is. In fact, in the United Kingdom manufacturers' advertising for consumer goods now amounts to less than 40% of the total.

That completes our working definition: 'An advertisement is a paid-for communication intended to inform and/or influence one or more people'.

What is advertising for?

Another boringly obvious question, you may think: everyone knows that advertisements merely exist to help people sell things to other people. Yet is it really so simple? What about Chuckles and M.—who was selling what to whom, there? When charities advertise for funds, what are they trying to sell? In Britain and throughout the world there is a continuing and welcome growth in Public Service advertising—persuading people not to waste energy, not to smoke cigarettes, not to take drugs (or to seek medical help if, unhappily, they already do). There are advertisements promoting road safety and promoting the aims of foreign governments who feel misunderstood. There is a huge volume of recruitment advertising, aiming to find the best peg for each particular hole. In none of these cases could the prime purpose of the advertising be described as being *to sell things to people*. (Though in every case the advertisements are intended 'to inform and/or influence' which as we have seen, is by no means necessarily the same thing.)

To answer the apparently naïve question '*What is advertising for?*', we must look at the various faces of advertising. For advertising is not a simple, single homogeneous thing. Different advertisers have different aims; and the best way to define what advertising is for is to classify the seven categories of advertiser and examine their specific aims and objectives. Here, then, are the seven basically different types of advertising:

Manufacturers' Consumer Advertising
Retailer Advertising

Trade, technical and industrial Advertising
Financial Advertising
Recruitment Advertising
Classified Advertising
Government and Public Service Advertising

Let us first look at the relative size and importance of each of them. In Britain, the United States and certain other countries, the amount of money spent by advertisers on television and in the leading journals (but not most of the minor ones) is measured in detail by independent commercial organisations. They sell the results of their researches to anyone interested in buying the data. This means that any major advertiser can discover what other major advertisers are spending on television and in the press; or that any journal can find out how much advertising other journals are carrying.

For other advertising media, however (posters, cinema, radio and the rest, where in fact far less advertising money is spent), there is not sufficient demand to make detailed measurements of advertising expenditures worthwhile. However, in Britain a non-commercial body called the Advertising Association (AA)—whose organisation and functions will be described in Chapter 7—makes annual global estimates for these less important advertising media. These AA estimates, based on sample researches among manufacturers and on government statistics, have proved reliable and accurate over the years. So that now the AA's annual advertising expenditure figures are generally accepted in industry and by government economists as the basic data on advertising trends.

In 1976, the AA showed that the total amount of money spent on all advertising was £1,188,000,000, just 1.09% of the Gross National Product. (Advertising has fallen as a percentage of the GNP over recent years. Appendix I shows the percentage of the GNP spent on advertising in other leading

Western Countries.) In the U.K. the £1,188,000,000 was broken down between the various faces of advertising as follows:

TABLE I

	Total Expenditure £ million	Percentage of the total
1. Manufacturers' Consumer Advertising	493	41%
2. Retail Advertising	206	17%
3. Trade, Technical and Industrial Advertising	130	11%
4. Financial Advertising	44	4%
5. Classified Recruitment Advertising	79	7%
6. Other Classified Advertising	135	12%
7. Government and Public Bodies' Advertising	45	4%
Other* Advertising	56	5%
	£1,188m.	100%

[Source: AA, 1976]

* 'Other' includes a large variety of comparatively small, miscellaneous advertisers including charities, foreign governments etc.

Thus we now have a clear picture of the relative size and importance of each of these sectors of advertising. In Chapter 2 we shall examine in detail how each functions, but let us first look briefly at their differing aims and objectives.

1. Manufacturers' Consumer Advertising (MCA)

Manufacturers' advertising of consumer products is, as we have seen, what most people think of as 'advertising' and it is indeed the largest single sector in expenditure terms. Nevertheless, its share of total advertising has fallen over recent years, as is shown by the following figures:

TABLE 2

Manufacturers Consumer Advertising (MCA)

	1971	1972	1973	1974	1975	1976
Percentage of Total U.K. Advertising Expenditure	46%	44%	41%	39%	40%	41%

[Source: AA]

Why should this have happened? To answer, we must first look at a brief history of manufacturers' advertising, particularly from the second half of the nineteenth century onwards.

In Britain, the United States and throughout Western Europe, in the second half of the nineteenth century three major developments took place simultaneously which together influenced the form and shape of modern advertising. These three developments were firstly the growth of industrial manufacturing companies, companies which initially specialised in the production and sale of a few similar products, whether soaps or foods or patent medicines or automobiles, which they manufactured in huge numbers at a low price; secondly, the growth of a totally separate retail industry, which was generally segmented into a myriad of small outlets and where, at first, economies of scale did not appear to apply to any significant extent; and thirdly, increasing wealth and changes in government legislation improved educational standards and increased literacy to such an extent that in Britain by 1880, according to the 1881 Census, about 80% of the population could at least sign their name, compared with only 60% thirty years previously.

How did these three developments interact and effect advertising? The most important of them, without question, was the first. A century before, Adam Smith, the founding father of modern economics, had shown that specialisation of labour and mass-production of goods would almost invariably lead to economies of scale and thus to lower costs and lower prices. Throughout the nineteenth century industrialists and businessmen proved in practice the validity of Adam Smith's theories, as they increased the size of their factories and produced ever-increasing numbers of products at lower unit costs. However, to justify the size of their factories the manufacturers desperately needed two things: mass national consumer demand and, so far as possible, stable (or better still, increasing) consumption of their products.

How were they to achieve these twin objectives, particularly when they did not own or control the large numbers of small retailers who sold their goods? One method was to by-pass the retailer and use their own representatives to sell their goods direct to the public. Some manufacturers tried this, and a few still do it today. Generally, though, using salesmen to call and sell direct to the public is more expensive than selling through retailers. There are exceptions to this rule of economics, but they are few. The reason is obvious: the retailer's shop stands still, and the customers do all the time-consuming and expensive travelling to and fro. If the customer stays still, at home, the sales representative must do the time-consuming and expensive travelling —which, in the long run, the customer must pay for. That is why, if you can compare price for price (which is not always easy), goods bought from direct salesmen are almost invariably *more* expensive than goods of the same quality bought from retail outlets.

This fact was crucial to the growth of manufacturers' consumer advertising. For when manufacturers realised that they could not use their own representatives to contact economically all the millions of customers they needed to achieve mass-production and continuous output, they searched for another answer to the problem of communicating with their customers. That answer was advertising.

However, advertising would not have been an effective answer had it not been for the simultaneous growth in education that occurred from the mid-nineteenth century onwards. In 1870 the British Government passed an Act which legislated for the provision of a school within reach of every child in the country. Elementary education became compulsory in 1880 and free in 1891. It became difficult for any child in Britain, even the poorest and most neglected, to escape altogether from schooling. And even though there might be as many as sixty in a class, and even though parents often connived in their children's truancy by sending them to work and earn money, the resulting improvement in literacy meant that advertisements could be published in the mass-media—and read by those very same millions of potential customers to whom the manufacturers wished to extol the virtues of their products.

The results of this increase in literacy and education were reflected in the growth of popular magazines and mass-circulation newspapers. Until 1855 newspapers in the United Kingdom were taxed, deliberately to make them expensive. There were separate newspaper stamp duties, advertisement duties (on each advertisement carried), and paper duties. These duties were known as 'taxes on knowledge' and their purpose was quite blatantly to prevent the poor and ill-educated from reading and learning about matters which they would not properly understand! So *The Times* cost 4*d*. (in 1855) and *The Guardian* 5*d*. (in 1851); and no daily had a circulation exceeding 50,000.

As soon as the notorious stamp duty was removed in 1855, newspaper prices fell to 1*d*. per copy. Circulations, of course, increased and new newspapers were launched. However, it was not until the 1890s that Alfred (later Lord) Harmsworth recognised and capitalised upon the potential inherent in the social and economic changes that had occurred. In 1896 he launched the *Daily Mail*. Immediately it reached a circulation of 200,000. By 1900 its circulation was running at an average of 989,300 copies per day.

The booming newspapers and magazines relied upon advertisers to subsidise their publications and thus keep down the cost to their readers. Likewise the advertisers were only too pleased to see the circulations of the media increase as their prices stayed low and more and more people—potential customers all—bought them.

That then, in very brief outline, is the history of why and how manufacturers began to advertise their goods in the mass-media.

The story was much the same in the United States and in Western Europe, though the growth of advertising in those countries in the nineteenth century lagged behind that of Britain. This was due to the fact that the Industrial Revolution occurred first in Britain and because the British national press grew and developed more rapidly than that of any other country.

Today the situation is more complex: there are many more media in which to advertise, and the economic strength of retailers has radically changed. In Chapter 2 we shall examine the role of Manufacturers' Consumer Advertising in the modern economy in much greater detail. However, manufacturers' objectives have not fundamentally altered over the last century: manufacturers advertise mostly in mass-media, in order to create mass consumer demand to achieve large-scale production, economies of scale, lower unit costs, and thus better quality goods and services at low prices.

2. Retailer advertising

As we have seen, retailer advertising has been rapidly growing in Britain. This trend has also occurred throughout the world. Indeed Britain is, if anything, some way behind other affluent nations in retail advertising. Below is a table showing what percentage of grocers, in countries throughout Europe, use advertising to promote their retail sales.

While every individual economist has his own list of which European countries have the most advanced and effective business management techniques, on most people's lists Sweden, Holland, Switzerland and Germany would be near the top, while Ireland, Italy and Spain would come near the bottom. And it may be no accident that the order in the table on the following page bears a close resemblance to most economists' tables of national business efficiency.

TABLE 3

	% of grocery stores using advertising extensively
Sweden	91
Holland	81
Switzerland	81
Germany	73
Austria	67
Belgium	58
Great Britain	51
France	44
AVERAGE	*44*
Ireland	38
Italy	18
Spain	6

[Source: AA, 1975]

This is because the last twenty years have seen a remarkable change in the structure of retail trading in all advanced economies. Retailers have organised themselves into major national chains; they have learned how to use their floor and counter space to maximise sales, and they have learned how to use their massive purchasing power to squeeze concessions from manufacturers. It is difficult to pinpoint why these developments have occurred comparatively recently, rather than before. Nobody knows the precise answer, but some of the forces which have helped to bring about the situation include:

Rapidly increasing shop rents, which have forced retailers to maximise their use of space and often forced smaller traders out of business.

Increased mobility of customers, making it possible for everyone to shop in town centres rather than in more expensive local stores.

Retailers' growing understanding that their closeness to their customers makes it possible for them often to dictate to manufacturers precisely what the customers want, and thus almost to control the manufacturers' production.

These and other forces have combined to produce the 'Retail Revolution' which has resulted in perhaps a couple of dozen retail names dominating British shopping habits—Tesco, Fine Fare, Sainsbury, Boots, Marks and Spencer, Woolworth, Littlewoods, Mothercare, W. H. Smith's and the rest.

At first these retail chains indulged in comparatively little advertising, relying on their High Street positions, their low prices and their window posters to bring in the customers. As the situation between them has grown more fiercely competitive they have realised, in common with retailers in Europe and the U.S.A., that they need advertising just as much as manufacturers do. The result has been a 70% growth in the share of advertising attributable to retailers between 1969 and 1976—from just under 10% to 17%.

However, retailers' advertising is characteristically quite different from manufacturers' advertising. Retailers' advertising is more strongly locally biased, since it needs to persuade customers to go to particular shops in particular streets; it also tends to be more *price* competitive, since most retailers in any field sell much the same products (often precisely the same brand, the *only* difference being price). Finally, retailers generally use the press media more than television, whereas in the case of MCA it is the reverse.

Since it is most likely, particularly in the light of the European figures quoted above, that retail advertising will continue to grow and grow over the next decade, we shall devote much attention to it in later sections of this book.

3. *Trade, technical and industrial advertising*

Trade, technical and industrial advertising is one part of the iceberg that the great majority of housewives, students and others hardly ever come across and know little or nothing about. Nevertheless, approximately £130,000,000 per year is being spent on it, accounting for 11% of the total. Moreover, in some ways this percentage figure underestimates its importance to the economy as a whole.

For trade, technical and industrial advertising (TTI) is the means by which companies introduce and promote their products to other companies. To do this they use some 2,000 journals, most of them highly specialised, plus direct mail. Many of the journals carry far more advertising than editorial matter, and this in itself is a reflection of the use that people in industry make of this type of advertising: the readers of the magazine do so partly in order to look at the advertisements.

This may seem surprising. You might expect most people to know the products which could help in their jobs, without the need for advertising. But *how* do they know? How can they find out about the innumerable technological developments, large and small, that go on throughout industry, inexorably and continuously? Sometimes they learn by word-of-mouth recommendation, sometimes by visits from sales representatives; most of all they learn from advertisements in their own trade, technical and industrial journals. Thus these journals, and this type of rather specialised advertising, genuinely and clearly help commerce and industry to function more knowledgeably and more efficiently. This is perhaps reflected in the fact that TTI, trade technical and industrial advertising, is highly developed and unquestioningly accepted even in planned, socialist economies.

4. Financial advertising

Although financial advertising is traditionally defined as one sector of total advertising—equivalent to approximately 4% of the total—it is in reality made up of two quite distinct segments. Both, naturally, involve advertising concerned with money; but their purposes are entirely different. The first segment should perhaps be treated as a sub-sector of trade, technical and industrial advertising, since it comprises advertisements run by companies primarily to communicate with other companies, usually with the aim of raising capital either now or in the future. In this way companies use advertising to communicate with the financial institutions—merchant banks, stockbrokers, insurance companies and so on. However, because these same advertisements are also usually intended to influence the private investor, and because they generally appear in public media such as *The Financial Times* and *The Times*, they are not grouped with TTI advertising.

Instead, they are grouped with the second segment of financial advertising which more directly addresses itself to the public at large. This is advertising which either seeks to obtain money *from* the public or loan money *to* the public. Some advertisers only raise money from the public and dispose of the funds themselves: examples are unit trusts, national savings, local government authorities and property funds. Some raise funds privately and only advertise to find borrowers: examples are second mortgage companies and money lenders. Most financial advertisers, however, borrow *and* loan money, so that sometimes they are advertising to raise funds, while at other times they will be promoting their borrowing facilities. The type of advertising they will concentrate on, at any particular time, will depend upon the underlying monetary trends in the economy. Examples of this type of advertiser are banks, building societies, financial brokers and, in a slightly different way, insurance companies. (Insurance companies advertise for you to place money with them now which they invest and then return to you when a specific event occurs e.g. on retirement, illness, accident or death.)

Both segments of financial advertising, and therefore the total sector, are among the most volatile parts of advertising. They tend to increase rapidly, almost frenetically, when the economy goes through an upsurge. Then everybody, including much of the public, busily trades in money, and tries to make a profit out of investing or borrowing. When the economy goes into even a slight decline, financial advertising tends to decrease quite quickly, as money becomes tight and profits become much harder to make. In the late 1950s and 1960s in both Britain and the United States financial advertising experienced an apparently irreversible boom. Inevitably the trend eventually reversed, and since then the volume and importance of financial advertising have declined considerably. Nevertheless, it still accounted for some £44,000,000 in the U.K. in 1976.

5. Recruitment advertising

Like financial advertising, recruitment advertising tends to reflect the volatility of the economy, but the oscillations are less violent. Once again recruitment advertising grew rapidly during the late 1950s and 1960s; it has however declined in recent years to the point at which its share represents only 7% of the total. Note that this figure accounts only for *classified* recruitment advertising. *Display* recruitment advertising—which is almost exclusively run by the government and nobody else—is treated separately.

Together with other classified advertising, recruitment advertising is one of the easiest faces of advertising to understand. Almost everybody has at one time or another tried to get a job, and looked at the recruitment advertisements in the process. And remember that by no means all (or perhaps even most) recruitment advertisements appear in the media. Signs outside factories ('*Fitters wanted*'), outside office blocks ('*Secretarial Vacancies*'), on local posters and in shop windows are all ways of bridging the supply and demand gap between employers and employees. In London's Soho there is a shop which specialises in carrying recruitment notices in its windows just for the tailoring trade—so that both employers and employees in the trade know precisely where to place their ads and where to look.

This interestingly demonstrates the most vital art (and science) in recruitment advertising. Whereas the aspects of advertising that we have considered previously address themselves to thousands—or even millions—of prospective readers and customers, classified recruitment advertisements are generally aimed at far fewer people: dozens or hundreds at the most. (It is an old joke of recruitment advertising that the *perfect* recruitment advertisement would

produce the single right reply from the one perfect applicant who is precisely and exactly right for the job—perhaps a sound objective to set when planning recruitment advertising, but patently unachievable!) Nevertheless, the fact that this type of advertising is addressed to tiny numbers of people means that it inevitably involves tight disciplines which we shall examine further in the next chapter.

6. Other classified

If total advertising has seven faces, then classified must have
about seventy! Even more than recruitment, it is an aspect
of advertising which everybody understands and knows
something about. This is because so much of it is placed
privately by individuals, rather than going through the
advertising industry as such. Individuals place all Births,
Marriages and Deaths classifieds, most Personal, For Sale
and Wanted classifieds, and a high proportion of Car,
Property and Holiday classifieds. Since this book is mainly
concerned to help students learn the business of professional
commercial advertising, we will not dwell too long on this
multi-faceted private advertising; but we should never forget its importance as a major source of revenue to press
media—£135,000,000, approximately 12% of the total in
the U.K. in 1976. Additionally, certain industries and companies use classified advertising extensively (estate agents,
car dealers, and travel companies particularly) and to these
we will return briefly later.

7. Government and public bodies' advertising

The government is far and away the largest advertiser in
Britain. Perhaps this is not surprising when you realise that
more than half of the Gross National Product is now
attributable to the public, or state-controlled, sector of the
economy, while less than half is still in the hands of the
private sector. The government spends £22,000,000 directly,
and £23,000,000 through such public bodies as the Butter
Information Council, Eggs Authority, Milk Marketing
Board and Dairy Council—making £45,000,000 in all,
accounting for 4% of the total in 1976. (In the United
States the government is the tenth largest advertiser, and
spent $113,000,000 in 1975.) All of government advertising
can be sub-divided into three parts:

1. *Recruitment*—mainly for the armed services, but also
   for nurses, police etc.

2. *Informative*—letting the public know factually about changes in legislation (e.g. decimalisation, metrication etc.).
3. *Persuasive*—intended to change the public's attitudes and actions for the national good (e.g. road safety, energy conservation, 'drink more milk' etc.).

Advertising placed by the government is, quite rightly, subject to certain requirements and constraints that commercial advertisers can ignore. For example, a manufacturer launching a new toilet soap may deliberately choose only to advertise in certain publications—those most likely to be read by potential purchasers of his soap. Whereas the government publicising, say, metrication will aim to get its advertisements seen by *every* member of the population, despite the fact that this will inevitably involve great and sometimes wasteful expense (in pure advertising terms). In addition the content of government advertising is subject to even closer critical scrutiny by the public at large than the rest of advertising—and so government advertising must always aim to be 'whiter than white'.

To deal effectively with these special needs and demands the government has set up a special unit within the Central Office of Information to co-ordinate and control its advertising activities. Once again, we shall be looking at the way this works in greater detail in the next chapter.

Summary

You now have some idea of the scope and variety of advertising. Most important of all, you realise that the Coke and Kelloggs commercials on television are only a very small, if conspicuous, part of the total. At the end of the book there are questions taken from recent Advertising Certificate examination test papers, set by the Communication, Advertising and Marketing Education Foundation. This Foundation is the educational body authorised by all sides of the advertising and marketing industry to organise and supervise education for students. If you wish to find out more about the CAM Foundation—and if you want to make a career in advertising you would be well advised to do so—then write for the syllabus and details of courses to:

Communication, Advertising & Marketing Education
   Foundation Limited,
     Abford House,
      15, Wilton Road,
       London,
        SW1V 1NJ

Having read only the above introductory chapter, however, you are not yet quite ready to cope with CAM examination questions. Instead, if you want to exercise your mind try the following Think Exercises. There will be some at the end of most chapters. You do not need to write anything down, if you do not wish to; they are not a test, and there will be no marks. But if you are really interested in advertising you will enjoy doing them. They will stretch your mind—as advertising will; they should be fun to do—as advertising is.

Think Exercises

1. The government is considering nationalising the advertising industry. Devise the government's posters and television commercials to promote the idea, and others aiming to persuade public opinion that it would be an unnecessary and undesirable proposition.

2. You tell your 80-year-old uncle that you are going to work in advertising. He replies, 'If you want to be a salesman, why not be honest about it and get out on the road.' Try convincing him that there is a bit more to advertising than that.

3. 'In a perfect world advertising would be totally unnecessary. We would all know what was available and would

simply buy what we wanted without manipulation or persuasion,' a bearded young economist challenges you on a train. You've got just seven minutes before your station to convince him that he is wrong.

2

The 3-Way Structure of the Advertising Industry: The Advertisers

Having outlined briefly in Chapter 1 the seven faces of advertising, in this and the two following chapters we must examine the structure of the advertising industry, to discover in detail how it functions.

The industry is structured into three separate, generally non-overlapping parts:

A—Advertisers
B—Media
C—Advertising Agencies

The advertisers, as we have seen, are those companies, institutions and individuals who decide to advertise, and it is they who foot the bill. They pay, firstly, the media in which their advertisements appear, according to scales which each of the media fixes. And they pay, secondly, the advertising agencies who design, write and produce the advertisements. Only very rarely do advertisers own the media in which they advertise (Thomson Holidays advertising in Thomson-owned newspapers is an example); and only very rarely do advertisers design, write and produce their own advertisements (usually it is the smaller advertisers who do this, but some large stores like C & A also do so). Generally then, with a few special exceptions, the advertiser hires an advertising agency to produce his advertisements, and pays for the space or time, in journals or on broadcast media, in which his advertisements appear. That is the 3-Way structure of the industry.

This chapter is about the advertisers, and explains how each of the seven types of advertiser puts advertising to work.

1. Manufacturers' consumer advertising

For the manufacturer of consumer goods and services advertising is a part of his total *marketing* activity.

What is marketing?
Marketing is the total function of learning what customers want, getting it produced and selling it to them at a profit. That, as you can see, is a wide—almost all-embracing—definition. Hence marketing is seen today as an extremely important function in modern commerce and industry.

Shrewd businessmen have always, instinctively, been good at marketing. However, it is only during the last thirty or so years that marketing has been consciously distinguished from other business activities and defined as a separate discipline. As a result, almost every major company nowadays includes marketing executives at the highest levels. Indeed, it is increasingly common for marketing men to become managing directors and even chairmen of large organisations.

Let us return to the definition above, in order to specify precisely the areas that *marketing* encompasses. First, it involves learning what customers want—partly through experience, partly through intuition and partly through market research (which is one of the most fundamental spheres of marketing activity). Second, marketing involves getting what the customers want produced. The marketing executive is not directly responsible for production, of course (that is a production executive's responsibility); but he *is* responsible for ensuring that what is produced is what the customer wants and is prepared to pay for.

Finally, and this is where advertising enters the picture, marketing involves selling what has been produced to the customer, at a profit. In order to achieve his sales the marketing executive can use a wide variety of methods: price deals, salesmen's incentives, public relations, give-aways, advertising and many others. All of these sales activities will cost money, and so the marketing executive must decide which will achieve the best results at the least cost. Remember, he must sell the goods at a profit. Possibly the profit may not be generated immediately. Particularly when launching new products into highly competitive markets, companies frequently accept that no profits will be made until maybe three years after the start, in which case the marketing executive will budget for a loss in years 1 and 2. Over the long term, however, if the launch is to be a success the marketing executive must ensure that this initial loss is fully recouped and more. (It is child's play, when you think about it, to sell things if you do not need to make a profit. You can simply lower the price to almost nil—or give away a Rolls-Royce free to every customer!)

Thus *marketing* covers a broad spectrum of associated functions—of which advertising is but one.

Marketing Director's Job Responsibilities

Market Research	Product Development	Sales Force	Sales Planning & Forecasting	Public Relations	Merchandising	Advertising

Having put advertising into its marketing context, we are ready to examine how manufacturers of consumer products use advertising to achieve four key objectives:

(*i*) To launch a new product or service
(*ii*) To promote an existing product or service
(*iii*) To add value to a product or service
(*iv*) To generate direct response.

Let us consider each of these in turn.

(*i*) *To launch a new product*—Every year about 600 new grocery products are launched in the United Kingdom.

Likewise new confectioneries, new toiletries, new cosmetics and a host of other new goods and services are continuously being introduced. Obviously, housewives know nothing about them, until they are advertised. Having seen the advertising, each housewife decides whether or not she or a member of her family would like to try the product. If she tries it, and decides that she and/or her family like it she will buy again. If, on the other hand, the product does not live up to expectations she will make no further purchases. Many new products, about 25 % of those launched each year, fail as a result.

Launching a new consumer product is expensive. Consumers are generally conservative, and need to be convinced that a new product is better than the one they are currently using. After all, spending their money on something they have never tried before involves them in taking a personal financial risk, however small it may be.

A new cigarette or a new grocery brand may therefore have between £250,000 to £2 million spent on it in advertising. If the product fails, all of that money may be lost. So nowadays manufacturers are very cautious about launching new products. Usually they test them extensively through market research prior to the launch, giving samples to consumers and gauging their reactions. Then, if possible, to further minimise their financial risks they launch the product in one town only or a small area of the country. Since advertising costs are roughly proportional to the size of the population covered, a launch in an area covering say 5 % of the population will cost just a little more than 5 % of the national launch. Regional launches of this kind are called *test markets*.

The largest advertisers of branded consumer products almost invariably use *test markets*. Proctor & Gamble, for example, test-marketed their toothpaste *Crest* in the south of England for over two years before launching it nationally. Throughout that two years they were constantly checking consumer reactions to Crest and to its advertising, because they were unwilling to commit themselves to a highly expensive national launch until they were virtually assured of success.

In some cases, however, it is not possible to test-market a new product. This may be because the initial capital cost of producing the product makes it uneconomic to produce just a small run for test-marketing. Cars are a perfect example of this. Another instance will be where the product is a fashionable one. It is pointless to test a product one year which will be out of fashion the next. Cosmetics are a typical example. Test markets cannot be used if there is a danger of a competitor seeing your product in test, copying it quickly and stealing a march on you. Some years ago Limmits slimming biscuits did just this when Simbix test-launched a new product formulation in one area of the country. Finally, test markets cannot be used where the advertising media that are right for the product launch are only available on a national basis. This is particularly true for expensive products aimed at the AB social classes, which must advertise in prestigious national publications.

As well as using advertising to launch completely new products, manufacturers use advertising to announce modifications and improvements to existing products. The procedure here is much the same as for new products, except that less advertising money is likely to be spent, so the necessity to use inexpensive test markets is correspondingly less great.

(*ii*) *To promote an existing product*—While almost everybody understands the need for advertising to launch new products, many people cannot see why it is necessary for manufacturers to keep on promoting products which have been on the market for years. Surely it is wasteful, such critics argue, to keep on advertising Kelloggs Corn Flakes and Coca-Cola and Heinz Beans and Guinness when there is nothing new to say about them? Everyone knows about them and has tried them already.

In fact there are many reasons why manufacturers find it necessary to continue to advertise well-known products. The first, and most basic, is the fallibility of the human memory. Most people are not very interested in advertisements and quickly forget the vast majority of those they see. How many that you saw a year ago can you remember now? A handful. How many then can you remember from five years ago? Almost none. Yet each week over 1,000 commercials are transmitted on every commercial station in Britain and you are additionally exposed to several thousand press advertisements and posters. Obviously advertisements which have been totally forgotten cannot influence your buying decisions. And even advertisements which are half-forgotten, which you have to dredge your subconscious to recall, are unlikely to be as effective as those at the top of your mind.

The second reason for continuing to advertise existing products is that there are always new people entering the market. Babies are born, grow into children, children become adults, get married, settle down, grow older, retire. At every stage their tastes and needs change. A girl who hated beer last week suddenly discovers she has acquired a taste for it; men are not interested in petrol advertising until they buy their first car; married couples begin to notice baby product advertising as soon as the wife becomes pregnant. As we change we want to be informed of the products relevant to our particular requirements at that particular time.

A third reason for advertising existing products has only recently been established through fairly advanced market research. It is this: even if a consumer knows about and already uses a particular product or brand, advertising can jog his or her memory and increase the rate of use of that product. If a man sees a beer commercial on television he may be tempted to get up and raid the fridge; if a woman sees a lipstick advertisement in a glossy magazine, she may be reminded to touch up her make-up. Obviously you cannot persuade people to do things that they do not wish to do, but these little memory jogs help to increase the consumption of advertised products and thus help to increase sales.

(*iii*) *To add value to a product*—Launching new products and promoting the sales of existing products are two main reasons why manufacturers advertise their goods. Now we come to a third, rather different and rather more complex reason. This is to make their goods more attractive, more desirable, and to enhance their *brand image. Brand image* is a term frequently misunderstood and misused. Quite simply, it means the mental images and emotions that people inevitably associate with the brands they use. Let us take as an example an instant coffee such as Maxwell House. Maxwell House will have certain specific, physical and chemical characteristics, which will define its taste, colour etc. But human beings react to products not merely physically but also emotionally. (This phenomenon is not caused by advertising; it exists in societies where there is no consumer advertising of brands at all.) Thus consumers will *feel* certain emotions about Maxwell House. They may feel it is the kind of coffee young people drink, or rich people or fashionable people; they may feel it is too strong for them, or too harsh, or just right. All of these images of the brand can be influenced (but rarely fundamentally changed) by advertising.

In this way advertising helps build *brand images*. If the image of a brand makes it especially attractive or desirable this increases its value to the consumer. She (or he) will choose to purchase the brand with the image she likes, rather than another whose formulation may be almost identical but whose image she finds unattractive. This may all sound rather deep and devious, but really it is not. It would be cheaper to pack expensive perfumes in medicine bottles; it is not vital for our clothes to be available in different patterns and colours; we could no doubt obtain all the nutrition we want from a few pills and some roughage.

Such basic products might meet our basic functional needs, but we would gain no pleasure from their use. Pretty perfume bottles, attractive clothes and well-cooked food all add to our emotional gratifications, and increase the enjoyment and value of otherwise dreary goods. Advertising, by enhancing the *images of brands* makes us want to buy them, and increases the pleasure we get from using them.

(iv)   To generate direct response—The fourth type of advertising which manufacturers carry out includes elements of each of the first three types, but is nevertheless quite distinct in aim and function. This is *direct response advertising*: advertising which generates sales (or sales enquiries) directly from advertisements without the intermediary distribution activity of retailers or wholesalers or even, in most cases, salesmen. This is the most scientific and measurable of all types of advertising.

Comparatively few types of product are suitable for selling directly off advertisements. Most products are so inexpensive, for example, cans of soup or packets of biscuits, that the postage costs make it ludicrous to buy them by mail; some products are too expensive, for example refrigerators and motor cars which people generally want to examine closely before deciding to make a purchase. Other products involve wide varieties of shade or size (cosmetics or men's suits) and so must be inspected before purchase. There is also the fact that many customers *dislike* buying products by post and prefer to buy products which they have seen and touched, even if the product is perfectly suitable for direct selling off advertisements.

Nevertheless, there are many products which can be, and are, sold effectively 'off the page'. The postal bargains pages in newspapers carry a variety of such products each week. Typically they will be fairly standard products costing not less than £3.00 nor more than £100.00 and will be products which can be packed and posted fairly easily. Mostly they will not be products on general sale through retailers, because if the manufacturer sells his own goods direct to the public and undercuts his retailers' prices, they will not surprisingly soon cease to deal with him. (Whereas if he charges the same price as retailers or more, most people will prefer to buy from the retailer, where they can inspect the goods.)

Sometimes direct response advertisers do not aim to sell their goods immediately 'off the page' but instead solicit enquiries for further information, usually with a comprehensive brochure or catalogue. Such advertisers believe, or have learned from experience, that before people will be persuaded to buy their products they need to give much more information than can economically be included in an advertisement. However, sending out brochures and catalogues is obviously an expensive business and direct response advertisers usually try to avoid it if they can.

What makes direct response advertising more scientific than any other is that it is the only sphere of advertising where sales can be directly attributed to individual advertisements. Therefore the money brought in can be compared precisely with the costs incurred. It works like this: you may have noticed that every direct response application says 'Write to Department ABCI—of the Purple and Mauve Manufacturing Company'. Alternatively, if a coupon is used which the customer is required to fill in when making a purchase or an enquiry, the coupon will have been marked with a code number (e.g. XYZI). The important thing to know is that the advertiser changes the Department or coupon code number *every time he advertises*. Even if the same advertisement is used again and again he will change the code number every time it appears. In this way he will know exactly how much sales response each individual advertisement generates. He can then build up a table of results as shown on the next page.

Even from this fictitious example it is possible to draw certain conclusions. The *Sunday Clarion* is obviously a much better 'buy' for the Purple and Mauve Manufacturing Company than the *Daily Bugle*. The *Clarion* generates more

TABLE 1

Purple and Mauve Manufacturing Company
Direct Response Analysis

Paper	Code No.	Cost of advertise-ment	No. of orders	Value of sales	Cost per order	Cost per £100 sales
Sunday Clarion	C1	£100	50	£2,000	£2·00	£5·00
	SC2	£100	40	£1,500	£2·50	£6·67
	SC3	£200	80	£2,500	£2·50	£8·00
	SC4	£50	25	£600	£2·00	£8·33
Daily	DB1	£50	10	£200	£5·00	£25·00
Bugle	DB2	£80	20	£300	£4·00	£26·67

orders and higher sales, at a lower average cost. Moreover its average size of order (value of sales divided by number of orders) is also higher—and direct response advertisers always seek the highest possible size of average order as this reduces the postage and packing costs as a proportion of the total. Finally we see that in both papers diminishing returns appear to be occurring; perhaps the product being sold is a seasonal one and the end of the season is approaching; or perhaps the advertisements being used are getting worn out, as frequently happens in direct response advertising.

All of this can be deduced from the figures. However, so far we have not considered the *content* of the advertisements. An experienced mail order advertiser will not only be experimenting in different journals, he will also be experimenting with different advertisement approaches. He needs to take care, of course, because if he allows too many variables to influence the response he may not be able to draw definite, valid conclusions from the results. Nevertheless, the rule for direct response advertisers is: test, test, test. With continuous, planned testing knowledgeable direct response advertisers build up a data-bank of past results so that they can predict with remarkable accuracy the volume of sales that future advertisements will achieve. However, it is essential to emphasise that not even the wisest of direct response advertisers is infallible: changes in the weather, in markets, in fashions, in competitive advertisers' activity can upset even the most scientifically designed campaign. The results of advertising can never be consistently predicted without error.

That, for the moment, completes our discussion of Manufacturers' Consumer Advertising—the largest single sector of advertising and the sector that everyone automatically thinks of as *real* Advertising.

Now we must consider how advertising works for the other six faces of advertising.

2. Retailer advertising

Retailer advertising is different from manufacturers' advertising in three key ways:

> (*i*) it is generally *local*, referring to individual shops or small groups of shops;
>
> (*ii*) it is generally more *price* orientated;
>
> (*iii*) it is generally more *topical*.

(*i*) Retailer advertising *is local*. At first sight it may seem obvious that retailer advertising should be local rather than national. Clearly small local traders should advertise in journals covering only their catchment area: a butcher in Wigan would be wasting a fortune if he advertised in the *Daily Mirror*, 99.9% of whose readers live miles out of his area. Yet today many retailers run national operations, with outlets in every major town. Why should such a national retailer not advertise in the same way as a national manufacturer? In fact, to a limited extent national retailers *do* advertise nationally. You will see advertisements for Tesco, Fine Fare, Boots and the Co-Op fairly frequently on television and in the mass-circulation national newspapers—the *Daily Mirror* and *Sun* in particular. However, the bulk of even these national chains' advertising is in local media, for three reasons. First, they often run different cut-price promotions in different towns at the same time, because of varying stock levels and varying local situations. (Despite the fact that Britain is a small country, tastes for different products vary widely from region to region.) Second, local papers can highlight the actual address of the particular store concerned, which national media cannot do. Third, retailers usually aim to charge advertising costs against individual store's sales in order to obtain a positive (if not absolutely precise) indication of the sales generated by their advertising, and this can be done far more accurately on a local rather than a national basis.

There are several consequences of this emphasis on local advertising. Retailers tend to use the television medium less than manufacturers of consumer goods. Instead they use local newspapers and local commercial radio; they need larger, highly efficient advertising departments which can ensure that the right advertisements go to all the right newspapers, frequently over a hundred of them, at exactly the right time; they must budget for much higher production costs for all of these different advertisements than the national advertiser who may produce just one colour advertisement and run it for a year. Because of these technical problems retailer advertising demands special expertise, and as a result certain individuals and agencies have become specialists in it.

(*ii*) Retailer advertising *is price orientated*. Look at some retailer advertisements. You will see that each typically comprises a lot of little sections, each one mentioning a particular product or brand at a special, low price. Retailers vie with each other to offer the lowest prices. To achieve these prices they drive very hard bargains with manufacturers, using their strength as *bulk buyers* to force the manufacturers to accept a lower price in return for a large contract. (It is of course this power to buy in bulk which has helped the national chains build up the size of their businesses at the expense of small traders, who cannot exert the same leverage on manufacturers and who therefore cannot offer such keen prices to their customers.) Having negotiated their sharp prices, the retailers must let the public know about them, and that is why their advertising is so price-orientated.

Because retailers frequently promote famous name brands in their advertisements, they sometimes seek to obtain a subsidy from the makers of the brand towards the cost. This is a matter for negotiation. The manufacturer will be more willing to contribute to the advertisement if he has not already been squeezed to supply his goods at a knock-down price. He may haggle with the retailer by offering to pay a considerable sum towards the combined advertising, if he can obtain a better profit margin on the sale price of his goods in return. This type of joint retailer/manufacturer advertising is called *co-operative advertising*. As well as being used by national grocery and chemists' chain stores, it is used extensively by the consumer durable industry, particularly the automobile industry. In this situation the automobile dealer will, as part of his contract with the manufacturer, undertake to advertise the maker's cars on a shared cost basis. The exact proportion paid by each party varies from manufacturer to manufacturer, and larger successful dealers may be able to obtain better terms than smaller ones. It is interesting that in co-operative advertising run by High Street retail chains the actual advertisements are almost always produced and organised by the retailer's advertising agency; whereas in the case of automobiles and consumer durables, the production of co-operative advertisements is invariably the responsibility of the manufacturer.

It is worth noting here that some major retailers run virtually no advertising. Marks and Spencer is the prime, famous example. Such retailers feel it unnecessary to advertise because they do not offer the same goods as other stores. Marks and Spencer, for instance, have all their merchandise manufactured to their own specifications. Thus the public cannot really compare the price of M & S goods with the price of the same goods further up the High Street, since the same goods cannot be found anywhere else!

Nevertheless you will notice that even Marks and Spencer's advertising volume has begun to increase over recent years, as the High Street battle for customers has become ever more fiercely competitive.

(*iii*) Retailer advertising *is topical*. Retailer advertising is topical not in the sense that it refers to notable events on the calendar, but in the sense that it changes very frequently. This is largely the result of its price orientation. As they aggressively compete with each other for customers, retailers are forever adjusting their prices and advertising their keenest prices that week—which they hope their competitors cannot match. A secondary cause of the topical nature of retailer advertisements are seasonal changes themselves, which of course particularly affect clothing retailers.

The fast-changing nature of retailer advertising is another reason why it demands particular expertise (and often extremely long working hours!) of a kind quite different from other slower moving, less frenetic forms of advertising.

3. Trade and technical advertising

The aims and functions of trade and technical advertising are quite different again. The difference is highlighted by the fact that trade and technical advertising is often called *industrial* advertising. In some ways this is a better name for it, since it involves advertising to people at their work and communicating with them in their job functions rather than as individuals. The key facts about trade and technical (or industrial) advertising are:

> (*i*) it addresses people at work, not as consumers;
> (*ii*) it uses small-circulation, specifically targeted media.

Let us, as before, examine in detail the key facts.

(*i*) *Advertising to people at work*. The crucial difference between advertising to people at their work and advertising to people at home is that people at work are very rarely spending their *own* money. The consequences of this difference, so far as advertising is concerned, are very great.

Before a company or a government department decides to buy anything that involves a significant financial outlay—more than a few paper clips or elastic bands—several people with quite different job functions are likely to have a finger in the decision. In industrial marketing and advertising these people are known as:

> The specifier
> The buyer
> The authoriser
> The user

In a small company, perhaps a one-man-band, all four functions may be carried out by a single person; in medium-sized companies two or three people will be involved; but in the largest companies and in government departments the four job functions will almost invariably involve four or even many more individuals.

Typically, the *specifier* will be a manager or department head, who will specify that Product X is needed and should be used in his section. His request will go to the buying department, where a *buyer* will first question whether or not Product X is needed at all. If he is convinced, and if the funds are available, it will be his job to obtain Product X at the lowest possible price. Depending on the magnitude of the cost of Product X, the buyer may be able to authorise the purchase himself or he may need to submit it to an *authoriser*, usually a director or managing director of the company, frequently (particularly in governmental bodies) a committee. Product X having been at last duly authorised, it is then ordered and on arrival the *users*—who work in the section under the manager who specified it—will put it to use.

Now clearly this complex process is quite unlike the 'at home' purchase situation where usually only one person, or at the most two, are involved. Moreover the attitude to Product X of the *specifier*, the *buyer*, the *authoriser* and the *user* may often be quite different; they may even be opposed to each other. The *specifier* will want the best quality product available, regardless of the cost; the *buyer* will want the cheapest, and will tend to minimise the differences between different qualities; the *authoriser* will be thinking of the long-term financial situation; and the *user* will not surprisingly want the product that makes his working life easiest and most pleasant. The trade and technical advertiser will therefore need to be both skilful and careful. And he will need to devise advertisements approaching each of the purchasing groups in their own terms, putting forward to buyers, for example, the facts and arguments that are relevant to buyers and not, perhaps, to specifiers or users.

(*ii*) *Using specifically targeted media.* The industrial advertiser is, fortunately, greatly helped in resolving the above problems by the existence of over 3,000 trade and technical publications each of which is aimed at a narrowly defined audience; and also by direct mail advertising.

Trade and technical publications can be broadly divided into two groups, sometimes called *horizontal* and *vertical* groups. The *horizontal* publications are published for people working in particular jobs, no matter what industry they work in. Examples are *Purchasing News* (for purchasing managers), *Safety Officer* (for safety and hygiene officers) and *Industrial Equipment News* (for industrial buyers). The *vertical* publications cover particular industries and aim to interest everyone working in that industry whatever their job function. Examples are *Timber Trades Gazette*, *Off-Licence News*, *Farmers' Weekly* and literally thousands of others. The advertiser can thus select his audience with some degree of precision and, for example, reach *buyers* through their publications and *specifiers* through theirs. Of course there is considerable overlap, since a buyer in a particular industry is likely to read both his own *horizontal* job function magazine and also the industry's *vertical* magazine. And the industrial advertiser must carefully take all of this into account when he plans his campaign.

It is partly because of this problem of overlap that industrial advertisers use *direct mail* advertising so much. *Direct mail* advertising, through the post, enables the advertiser to reach whoever he wants, when he wants, without the possibility of surrounding editorial articles distracting the reader from his message.

Several companies exist which specialise in handling direct mail advertising. They have lists of hundreds of thousands of addresses stored on computers so that an advertiser can obtain the addresses of precisely the people he wants to reach. Often the addresses are listed by name, otherwise merely by job description ('The Finance Director, Purple and Mauve Manufacturing Company Limited' etc.). Obviously letters personally addressed by name are far more likely to be read by the recipient than mere anonymous missives. However, such personal lists are far more expensive to use due to the high costs both of compiling them and of keeping them up-to-date when individuals change their companies and their jobs.

Indeed high cost is the prime disadvantage of direct mail advertising. As postage rates continuously rise, it can cost £150 or more per 1,000 direct mail shots, compared with maybe £10 per thousand individuals reached via trade magazines. The other disadvantages of direct mail advertising are that it is known to antagonise some recipients; that often it is opened by secretaries and thrown into the wastepaper basket unseen by the addressee; and that it does not have the 'authority' of advertisements surrounded by informative editorial material in magazines. Thus before deciding in any particular instance whether to use publications or direct mail, the industrial advertiser in consultation with his agency must weigh up the pros and cons of each. It can be a difficult decision to reach.

Finally there is a sector of trade advertising which is

different from all previously described; trade advertising aimed principally or exclusively at retailers. This is by no means so complex or so specialised as industrial (or technical) advertising, and it is undertaken by companies who manufacture consumer goods and wish to persuade retailers to buy-in and stock those goods. Such advertising, which is almost a sub-section of manufacturers' consumer advertising, is normally produced by the same agencies and people and at the same time as the consumer campaign. The publications used are self-descriptive: *The Grocer, Supermarket News, Retail Chemist, Travel Trade Gazette* and so on. And the message of such advertising is always the same, no matter how cleverly disguised it may be: if you stock our product, your shop will make more profit. Many companies doubt whether such advertising is truly cost-effective; but others believe in it passionately, and there are no scientifically conclusive facts either way.

4. Financial advertising

As we saw in Chapter 1, the section defined as *financial advertising* embraces a heterogeneous group of sub-sections of which the key ones may be classified as:

> (*i*) *Advertising for money;*
> (*ii*) *Advertising to loan money;*
> (*iii*) *Insurance advertising;*
> (*iv*) *Prospectuses and shareholder advertising.*

(*i*) *Advertising for money*—The leading institutions advertising for public money are Banks, Building Societies, National Savings, Local councils and Unit trusts and bonds. For each of these the advertising has a different function. *Banks*, as well as seeking to persuade the public to deposit money with them, also offer a wide range of financial services on which they make a profit. Moreover, the services which each of the leading banks offers vary in detail from bank to bank and each of the banks will therefore promote its particular services as a way of persuading customers to deposit their accounts with them. *Building Societies* on the other hand almost always offer precisely the same interest rates and services. Building Societies therefore compete among themselves by promising to be more reliable and sometimes a bit friendlier than each other.

Both banks and building societies share an advantage over other financial institutions: they both have 'retail outlets' on the High Street where you can go to discuss your financial problems and gain reassurance.

National Savings (and Premium Bonds) sells its 'products' through post offices but these are not equipped to handle general financial problems. National savings and premium bonds, therefore, generally aim to offer excellent tax-free monetary returns. *Local councils* have no retail outlets at all, and therefore rely on offering the highest possible interest rates, usually in small space advertising, relying on their official status to reassure prospective investors about their probity.

Finally, *Unit trusts and bonds* are, comparatively speaking, young upstarts in the world of financial advertising: the oldest unit trust in the U.K. is just over 40 years old. They too have no High Street 'retail outlets' where customers can come to learn more (though some do employ sales representatives). Faced with these sales difficulties unit trusts and bonds have generally used *direct response* advertising, selling their investment 'off the page', with large spaces in which they publish a lot of reassuring and informative factual detail. Nevertheless despite the considerable weight of advertising put behind unit trusts over the last twenty years, less than 5% of the population have any money in this form of investment, and these are drawn almost exclusively from the wealthier social classes (the ABs).

(*ii*) *Advertising to loan money.* This is a much smaller segment of financial advertising, and we need not go into too much detail here. The main advertisers are authorised money lenders, who invariably use classified advertising; second mortgage companies, who loan money to house owners guaranteed by a second mortgage on their house—a risky form of borrowing no longer very popular; hire purchase companies, who likewise advertise comparatively little today, preferring to sell their HP contracts at the place where people buy the goods involved; and banks, who promote borrowing as part of their overall financial service. Times change of course and advertising to loan money may grow in importance in the future, but at the moment such a prospect is not foreseeable.

(iii) *Insurance advertising*. Insurance companies, on the other hand, are quite heavy advertisers. Insurance business is in two parts: (a) risk insurance and (b) life and pensions insurance. The fundamental difference is that risks may *never* occur, whereas all of us *will* die one day. Within the insurance companies these two types of business are treated separately, and this is reflected in insurance companies' advertising. Most insurance company advertising is on the life and pensions side. There are two main reasons for this. First, it is basic business that insurance companies want, because it is steady and actuarially highly predictable whereas 'risk business' is, in a word, much more risky! Second, although certain highly specialised types of risk insurance (like shipping and art coverage) are big business, the type of risk policy which the general public takes out is usually quite small and thus less profitable than life and pension insurance.

If you study both risk and life insurance advertisements you will quickly spot that they all can be split into two almost opposite approaches. Either they delicately point out the dire consequences of not taking out insurance (the 'fear motive') or they emphasise the enjoyment that well-planned insurance can bring, particularly at retirement (the 'hope motive'), the two opposite themes neatly symbolising the two underlying reasons why people take out insurance policies. Thus these approaches are built upon peoples' real needs and desires, which as we shall see when we come to Campaign Planning (Chapter 5) is the basis for all effective and successful advertising.

(*iv*) *Prospectuses and shareholder advertising.* In the United Kingdom—and indeed in the United States and throughout Europe—the laws governing the issue and sale of company shares are most strict. In the nineteenth century unscrupulous semi-criminal (or sometimes wholly criminal) financiers raised money from trusting members of the public by floating sham companies. Once the public had put their money into these companies, the financiers were able to use the funds for their own purposes, occasionally absconding with everything. To put a stop to such unacceptable practices governments and stock exchanges drew up stringent regulations specifying the information which all share prospectus advertisements must carry, including a history of the company, the names and addresses of its directors and their shareholdings, and every other significant fact. As a result share prospectus advertisements are packed with small type and look rather uninviting. Those involved in their preparation tend to be specialists working in specialist financial agencies, who know all the legislation inside out, and can be relied upon to ensure that the advertisements they produce carry no mistakes.

In addition to share prospectuses, companies often run advertising publicising their annual trading results. These annual report advertisements are aimed at existing shareholders, prospective shareholders and the financial institutions. While the regulations governing them are laxer than those for prospectuses, these advertisements too must be especially carefully worded and supervised. Generally they are produced by the same specialist financial agencies that produce prospectus advertisements. There are about two dozen such financial agencies in the U.K. and predictably most of them are to be found in or near the City.

5. Classified advertising

Excluding recruitment (which will be dealt with in the next section), the great bulk of classified advertising is placed by individuals and so is of no professional concern to those whose career is in advertising. The key areas in which professional and commercial advertising skills are sometimes brought to bear are:

> (i) Holiday advertising;
> (ii) Motor car advertising.

(i) *Holiday advertising*—Again, many holiday advertisers are either individuals offering their caravans or chalets to let, or one-man-band travel operators who write and place their advertisements themselves. However, large national holiday companies also use classifieds, often in addition to large space display advertisements. Why do they use both?

One of the most basic questions which any advertiser needs to resolve before spending his money on advertising—and which we shall return to when analysing Campaign Planning in Chapter 5—is whether his prospective customers are conscious of their need for his type of product and are likely to be actually looking for it; or whether prospective customers are unaware that his product could benefit them and need this fact to be quite positively drawn to their attention. At one extreme will be, say, a new detergent—which nobody will be interested in until they have been fiercely convinced that it is demonstrably better than the many satisfactory powders already on the market. At the other extreme is the bicycle-buff who buys *Exchange and Mart* and diligently peruses its columns each week hoping to discover a secondhand penny-farthing of the Edwardian era. Broadly speaking, if what you are advertising is of the first kind you will need to advertise with large spaces or on television, aiming to ensure that even the most uninterested of prospective customers will notice your advertisement. If on the other hand what you are advertising is of the second kind you can use extremely small space advertisements or classifieds, which are of course much cheaper, and you rely upon the customer to search them out.

Holiday advertising requires an element of both approaches. Many holidaymakers plan their vacation well in advance, and will decide for themselves where they want to go, how they want to get there and how much they wish to spend. They then scan the classifieds to find the holiday which will best suit their requirements. Other holidaymakers, however, will be far less certain about precisely how they wish to spend their annual break. They are more likely to notice and be influenced by bigger advertisements which they were not consciously looking for, and they are less likely to rummage through classifieds. These then are the reasons why large national holiday companies choose to use both types of advertising.

Whichever they use, you will find that their advertisements almost always offer brochures and *carry key numbers*. Remembering what you learn about other *direct response* advertisers, you will be able to deduce exactly how and why holiday advertisers use these key numbers to their advantage.

(*ii*) *Motor car advertising*—Most classifieds for motor cars are for second-hand vehicles, although some are for the rarer new cars. Here classifieds are again functioning as an inexpensive way of reaching people in search of a particular type or price of car. Nearly all such advertisements are placed by dealers rather than by manufacturers. And the larger dealers almost always use professional advertising consultants—indeed they may be forced to do so if all or part of the cost is borne by the car manufacturer. This, and other local retail advertising, is the backbone of the out-of-London agency business, as we shall discover in Chapter 4.

Finally, one other type of commercial concern uses classifieds to a considerable extent: estate agents. However, largely for historic reasons almost every estate agency devises and places its own advertising without the aid of professional advice.

6. Recruitment advertising

Recruitment advertising is really another section of classified advertising. It therefore works in the way that other classified advertising does. It is also normally handled by specialists. The key reasons for this are that:

> (*i*) *Recruitment advertising is often placed by recruitment consultants;*
> (*ii*) *Recruitment advertising calls for different skills.*

(*i*) *Recruitment consultants*—A company seeking new staff via advertising, particularly senior staff, must go through five processes.

> (*a*) It must carefully define the job to be advertised;
> (*b*) It must plan and produce the advertising;

    (*c*) It must sift the written response and draw up a short list;

    (*d*) It must invite those on the short list for a preliminary interview;

    (*e*) It must finally re-interview the really probable applicants.

(Sometimes (*d*) and (*e*) can be compressed into a single interview, but usually not.) Clearly this procedure is extremely time-consuming and time costs money. Therefore many companies nowadays use the services of an independent recruitment consultant who, after a briefing, carries out processes (*a*) to (*d*) for a fee. As part of this fee payment the recruitment consultant will plan and produce the advertising (*b*).

In addition to recruitment consultants, a small number of advertising agencies specialise in recruitment advertising. In discussion with their client company they will supervise processes (*a*), (*b*) and sometimes (*c*); but they will be paid less than independent consultants and therefore do less of the work, so that the client company shoulders more of the burden.

(*ii*) *Recruitment advertising skills*—In some ways recruitment and retailer advertising are quite alike. Both frequently need to be planned and produced speedily, much of both is placed in local newspapers; both tend to carry lots of copy with little or no illustration. In these ways the knowledge and skills required by the recruitment and retailer advertising specialists are not dissimilar. But there is one marked dissimilarity: retailer advertising aims to sell goods to anyone with the money to buy; recruitment advertising aims to persuade just a few relevant applicants to apply. Therefore retailer advertisements need to be creatively persuasive, while recruitment advertisements must be much more plainly factual. Hence consultants and agencies specialising in recruitment do not normally employ highly-paid copywriters and art directors. Their skills are not needed. Indeed they would be misplaced. Great expertise is required in devising effective recruitment advertisements but the expertise needed is merely of a different, perhaps more disciplined nature than that needed in the production of other types of advertising.

7. Government advertising

As we saw earlier, government advertising in the United Kingdom (and abroad) has increased rapidly over recent years. In the U.K. it is centralised and co-ordinated by a government department called the Central Office of Information, and it can be divided into three key sections:

(*i*) Government recruitment
(*ii*) Government information
(*iii*) National needs

(*i*) *Government recruitment.* Why is government recruitment different from other recruitment? Firstly, because of its scale. Very rarely do companies ever want to recruit more than a few dozen people at a time whereas government seeks thousands, and even tens of thousands for the armed services, for nursing, and to a lesser extent for the police and nationalised industries. Secondly, and more importantly, government recruitment is different because these kinds of government jobs involve people (usually young people) in a total change of life-style. This is quite different from most commercial recruitment advertising, which deliberately seeks to find job applicants with relevant experience. A sales representative who changes his employment may have to move house, but he will still find himself doing the same kind of job, whereas the armed forces recruit people from all walks of life, totally without relevant experience (which of course is virtually impossible to obtain without joining the forces).

This brings us back to the distinction between small-space classified and large-space 'impactful' advertising. The commercial recruitment advertiser can rely upon the likelihood that people with the relevant experience who are looking for a job will notice his advertisement. The government has to persuade young people who probably have never seriously thought about joining the forces or becoming nurses to consider the possibility. This cannot be done effectively— and certainly not on the scale required—with small space classified advertising. Of course in some societies, the government might simply direct or force people into those areas of employment it wishes to see filled. But in our society, and in any free society, the government must seek to persuade. That is why they need to use advertising, one of the most effective means of persuasion known.

(*ii*) *Government information.* By no means all government advertising, though, is intended to be persuasive. Governments believe that they have a responsibility to communicate certain legislative changes factually and simply to the public. Well-known examples of such advertising campaigns in Britain have been these for decimalization and metrication; but there are many others going on continuously, particularly informing companies and employers of their responsibilities and rights under new Parliamentary Acts.

In some ways these campaigns spotlight the difficulty of differentiating between *persuasive* and *informative* advertising, even when the advertising concerned aims to be merely informative and hardly persuasive at all. For one thing, such advertisements always tend to look rather dull and uninteresting, almost as bad as share prospectuses (and for fundamentally the same reason, if you analyse it carefully), and even though they do not aim to persuade, the mere fact that they are published by the government gives them convincing authority. Lastly, the government inevitably wants the public to accept the legislation concerned, whatever it may be, and so describes it in an acceptable rather than disapproving way. Thus even the government's purely informative advertisements contain a persuasive element.

(*iii*) *National needs.* Government advertising to promote public action in the realm of 'national needs', on the other hand, could not be more persuasive in intent. This category covers campaigns for road safety, to conserve energy, to reduce smoking and even, in an unusual case in Britain, raising public support for an anti-inflation campaign.

Campaigns such as these fringe on the imprecise border between advertising and propaganda. This is partly because they sometimes involve issues upon which the whole nation does not agree. The British Government's anti-inflation policy, for example, obviously had political overtones which the advertising campaign promoting it tried hard, but not totally successfully, to avoid. Even energy conservation campaigns are unlikely to be wholeheartedly supported by people working in the energy-producing industries. Surprisingly, there appear to be no *statutory* limitations on the content of advertising that a British government might use to promote public acceptance of its policies. This is undoubtedly because governmental use of paid-for advertising has only recently become significant. Nonetheless, there is no known example of democratically-elected governments abusing their power in this respect. (Cynics argue that they are frightened to do so because when the opposition party takes over, maybe at the next election, it need then have no scruples about similarly misusing advertising as propaganda.)

Dictatorial governments, on the contrary, have no qualms whatsoever about using advertising and all the other techniques of mass persuasion at their authoritarian disposal. In fact, British governments take pains to avoid as far as possible political propaganda in their 'national needs' advertising (except in wartime, which is clearly a quite special situation). They also go to great lengths to ensure that their campaigns are, in economic terms, worth the money they cost. Through the Central Office of Information sophisticated market research is continuously carried out to discover what proportion of the public have seen the government's campaigns, what they understand by them and what action they have taken as a result of them. Thus in a famous study, published by the Advertising Association, it was shown that advertising to persuade people to wear seat-belts not only saved people's lives, but actually saved the country money in terms of hospitalisation costs, work days lost and disability pensions—far more than the campaign cost the government to run.

There is, of course, one form of advertising that is blatantly political in nature: pre-election campaign adver-

tising. Obviously this is spasmodic and compared with other advertising, little money is spent upon it. Moreover, in Britain only the Conservative party uses and pays a full-time advertising agency. The Labour and Liberal parties prefer to rely upon unpaid work by supporters who are, admittedly, usually professional advertising executives. (In the United States both parties, and some Presidential candidates, usually use paid advertising agencies—though the situation changes from election to election.) The ins and outs of pre-election campaigns have been discussed in many books, and we cannot begin to do justice to the subject here. Obviously it is an extremely important and fascinating area of advertising activity. Suffice it to say firstly that, despite often shrilly expressed fears to the contrary, no politician or party yet has even an inkling of how to plan anything like a guaranteed successful campaign, and secondly, that if you have political inclinations at all and are by chance lucky enough to get to work on a pre-election campaign, you will find it stimulating, exciting—and enjoy yourself immensely.

We have now completed our detailed analysis of why the different kinds of advertiser undertake advertising campaigns. It is, therefore, time to try and stretch your mind again with some Think Exercises. If you are going to do them, try hard. Remember that only you will know how much effort you have put into them.

Think Exercises

1. Try to think of three products which it would seem to make perfect advertising sense to sell via direct response advertisements 'off the page', but which you have never seen so advertised.

2. You have worked for five years in manufacturers' consumer goods advertising and now you've decided that you would like to work in retailer advertising. How would you convince your prospective employer at the

interview that, despite your lack of directly relevant experience, you are just the right person for the job? Imagine his probing questions, and your answers.

3. A new right-wing government Minister decides that it is in the national interest to reduce the power of Trade Unions. He asks the Central Office of Information to plan a campaign to build public support for his efforts. Imagine you are the senior civil servant at the COI and—without taking sides *pro* or *con* Trades Unions—try to persuade the Minister that it is wrong to use advertising in this way.

4. Now think of the reasons why it will be difficult to sell successfully via direct response advertising the products you chose for Question 1. (If they are not being sold that way already, there are almost bound to be some reasons why not!)

3

The 3-Way Structure of the Advertising Industry: The Media

We now come to the second separate part of the advertising industry: the media which carry the advertisements. As usual we must begin by carefully defining precisely what the 'media' are, especially since media has recently become something of a jargon word, much abused and misused. Media is of course simply the old Latin plural form of the singular noun medium, and in the Oxford Dictionary you will find the relevant definition of the noun medium as:

> 'Any intervening substance through which a force acts on objects at a distance or through which impressions are conveyed to the senses.'

Which is almost exactly what a medium is in advertising terms: 'Any intervening substance . . . through which impressions are conveyed to the senses.' The impressions are the advertisements, and these are conveyed to the senses through the media of newspapers, television, radio and the rest.

However, in advertising media, are of little significance unless they are mass media. This is because advertisers rarely want to communicate merely with one or two people; that job can be better performed by personal contact. Advertisers need to communicate with thousands or even millions of people. (Even recruitment advertisers usually need to communicate with many thousands of people in order to find the right ones for the job.) Thus, in order to be of importance to major advertisers, a medium will need to be able to convey advertisements to the senses of large numbers of people.

Of course, the advertiser will have to pay the media for carrying his advertisements. And this leads us to the two basic criteria by which the efficiency of all advertising media are judged:

> (*i*) How many people does the medium reach? (And if it is possible to find out, what kind of people are they?)
>
> (*ii*) How much does it cost to use the medium? (And compared with alternative media, is it the best possible value for money?)

To examine these questions we must now consider each of the main advertising media sectors, and the best way to start is by looking at their relative sizes in terms of the amounts of advertising money spent with each of them.

Total U.K. Advertising Expenditure by Media (1976)
(£ million)

Press and Magazines	£809
Television	£307
Poster and Transport	£43
Cinema	£8
Radio	£21
Total	£1,188

In the United States, the approximately equivalent figures were ($ million):

Press and Magazines	$10,447
Television	$4,851
Poster and Transport	$345
Cinema	$4,851
Radio	$1,837
Total	$22,331

[Source: IPA]

It will readily be seen that Radio advertising is proportionately far larger in the U.S.A. than it is in the U.K. This is due to the fact that there is a much greater number of local commercial radio stations in North America than in Britain. Expenditures for other leading countries are shown in Appendix III.

Returning to the U.K. situation, despite minor fluctuations from year to year each sector's share of the total has been remarkably constant for well over 15 years:

Percentage of Total U.K. Advertising Expenditure

	1960	1976
Press and Magazines	70·9%	68·1%
Television	22·3%	25·8%
Poster and Transport	5·0%	3·6%
Cinema	1·5%	0·7%
Radio	0·3%	1·8%
	100·0%	100·0%

[Source: Advertising Association]

However, despite their consistency there are underlying trends behind these figures:

1. A slow growth in the share of advertising held by the Press media, attributable entirely to a startlingly rapid increase in the volume of money being spent in regional newspapers. These now account for 27·6% of the total and hold the largest single slice of the total cake. If you have forgotten our earlier remarks about TV not being the all-important advertising medium, this fact may surprise you.
2. There has been a long-term decline in poster advertising's share of the cake, though this decline has stabilised over the last five years.
3. There has been a still longer-term decline in cinema advertising's share, and this decline has yet to be halted.
4. There has been a rapid recent growth in the volume of radio advertising, following the government legislation setting up commercial radio in 1974.

That is a bird's eye view of the overall media picture in Britain. Before we go on to examine each of the component

parts in detail, it is important to say that most of the information on advertising costs and circulations in this chapter
comes from a publication called *British Rate and Data*
(BRAD). BRAD is a 500-page compendium, published
monthly, which lists every significant advertising medium
in Britain. In addition to costs and circulations it gives
sizes, copy dates, printing processes and even the names of
the people working in the advertisement department of each
medium. It is probably the single most important publication for anyone working in advertising in Britain. If you
possibly can, look through a copy. Your public library may
have one. You will soon see how thorough and comprehensive it is. It has no competitor and is quite indispensable in
the planning of advertising campaigns.

Press and Magazines

The total figure of £809,000,000 spent on press advertising
in 1976 breaks down as follows:

| | Advertising Expenditure | |
	£ million	% of total advertising
National Newspapers	197	16·6
Regional Newspapers	328	27·6
Consumer Magazines	92	7·7
Trade and Technical Journals	103	8·7
Directories (incl. Yellow Pages)	31	2·6
Press, Production costs	58	4·9
	809	68·1

(*i*) *National newspapers.* The British national press has suffered
chronic economic problems for the last two decades, primarily as a result of its escalating costs and its slowly declining
share of the advertising cake. Nevertheless, it is still the
largest and strongest national press in the world and the
British are very fortunate to have so wide a variety of good
national newspapers from which to choose. Look at the
list:

National Dailies	Circulation 1976	National Sundays	Circulation 1976
Daily Mirror	3,831,708	News of the World	5,113,517
Sun	3,738,765	Sunday Mirror	4,035,661
Daily Express	2,556,396	Sunday People	4,019,819
Daily Mail	1,800,163	Sunday Express	3,406,500
Daily Telegraph	1,304,246	Sunday Times	1,414,304
Times	310,785	Sunday Telegraph	812,447
Guardian	300,282	Observer	656,220
Financial Times	175,999		
Morning Star	39,333		

[Source: BRAD]

This list excludes special interest dailies like The *Sporting Life*, the *Morning Advertiser* (the licensed trade's own daily paper), and Scottish dailies like *The Scotsman* and *Glasgow Herald*; even the immigrant Pakistanis have their own paper, *The Daily Jang.*

Remembering the two basic criteria on which all advertising media are judged, you will realise that circulation figures are exceptionally important to an advertiser. During the nineteenth century newspapers frequently lied about their circulations. There were instances of local papers selling space to advertisers and printing only two or three copies, especially to show the advertiser! Travel was then so difficult that an advertiser might find it all but impossible to journey to, say, Newcastle merely to check that the local paper was being printed and distributed properly. To put an end to such fraudulent practices the leading advertisers and publishers together set up an independent body called the *Audit Bureau of Circulations* which measures the sold circulation of every issue of any publication that wishes to join it. 'Unsolds', which are copies that the papers distribute but which are returned unsold, are not counted into the circulation; nor are copies given away. *The Audit Bureau of Circulations'* (always called ABC for short) figures have a long record of thorough accuracy and reliability.

Approximately 1600 publishers are members of the ABC. Others do not join, either because they do not want to pay the charges which the ABC levies to cover its costs, or because they feel that their circulations are too small to be worth measuring and publishing. Rightly or wrongly, many advertisers treat journals which do not join the ABC and publish its independently audited circulation figures with some suspicion, and tend to prefer not to advertise in them.

Why are the circulation figures so important? Because of course, together with the readership figures which we shall come to in a moment, they tell the advertiser what he is getting for his money. Let us examine this point by asking first how much it costs to advertise in a newspaper. The answer is surprisingly complicated. All newspapers charge different rates for different types of advertisement. But they always start with a basic *standard rate* which is the price they charge for one centimetre of space in one column of their paper. Here is a sample of *Single Column Centimetre* standard rates in 1976:

	S.C.C. rate
Daily Mail	£14·00
Daily Telegraph	£14·00
Guardian	£8·50
Sun	£20·50
Times	£9·00
News of the World	£23·00
Sunday People	£21·50
Sunday Telegraph	£9·00
Observer	£11·00
Sunday Times	£18·50

Excluding classifieds, the smallest display advertising space sold by newspapers is 3 single column centimetres. (In the United States space is sold not in single column centimetres but in *Agate Lines*. An *Agate Line* is one single column wide and $\frac{1}{14}$ inch deep. The smallest size sold is normally 14 *Agate Lines*, i.e. a 1-inch single column space.)

Having fixed its *standard rate*—which will of course change from time to time, particularly during periods of inflation— each newspaper then fixes its *special rates* for particular classes of advertiser. Some of the rates will be higher than the *standard rate*, some lower. This is a list of the situations in which *The Times* charges special rates:

Special positions (front page, for example)
Solus positions (only one advertisement on the page)
Women's pages
Book publishers
Charities
Entertainments (cinemas and theatres)
Share prospectuses
Large spaces (whole pages, for example)
Colour advertisements (highly expensive)
—and certain others.

The advertiser, in consultation with his agency, decides what size of space he will need to use, decides whether or not he wants it in a special position or on a special page, and then calculates the cost. Sometimes it will be vital for the advertisement to appear in one particular newspaper. More commonly the advertiser will have a choice of all the newspapers available.

Before making his selection of which to use he will calculate the price of the space required for each of them. Then he will divide the price of the space by the circulation of the paper in order to discover how much it is costing him to reach each thousand purchasers of the newspaper. Newspaper A may be charging a very high price for a small circulation, whereas newspaper B is charging a low price for a high circulation; in which case newspaper B will obviously be the much better bargain from the advertiser's point of view. This calculation of the *cost per thousand* circulation is of fundamental importance in advertising, and we shall return to it again when we analyse *Planning a Campaign* in Chapter 5.

Measuring the circulation of a journal gives only one half of the picture. It is just as important for an advertiser to know how many people actually *read* it, and who they are. This is because advertisers are primarily concerned, as we saw at the beginning of this chapter, with the *number of relevant people* who see their advertisement.

Let us examine this point further, since it is most important. Firstly, we all know that some publications have far more *readers per copy* than other publications. A monthly magazine like *Vogue* which may end up lingering for months in a dentist's waiting room, may well be seen by dozens or even hundreds of readers. A daily newspaper like *The Sun* on the other hand is likely to end up wrapping fish and chips after only one or two people have looked at it. A straightforward comparison of the *circulation* of *Vogue* and of the *Sun* would therefore be misleading. To the advertiser it is far less important how many people buy the publication than how many people see it—and see his advertisement within it.

Secondly, it is obviously vital to the advertiser that the people who see his advertisement should be *relevant*. There is no point in an advertiser conveying his messages to the senses of millions of people none of whom are relevant or could possibly be interested. For example, *Vogue* is read each month by over a million women, but it would not be the ideal place to advertise a handrolling tobacco or a new patent screwdriver. Equally *Practical Householder*, which has a similar *number* of readers would not be the ideal place to advertise Cardin suits or Givenchy perfumes. The advertiser thus wants to know, so far as possible, both how many people each medium reaches and what kind of people they are.

To ascertain the number of people who read each of the leading journals in the U.K. and to obtain an outline profile of who they are, the advertising industry sponsors a continuous major market research study called the *JICNARS* National Readership Survey*. This survey interviews approximately 15,000 people every six months and asks them which newspapers and magazines they read. More than 100 national publications are covered.

Having asked which publications each respondent reads, the interviewer also notes their age, social class, where they live, whether they watch ITV, whether they own cars, pets,

---

* JICNARS stands for Joint Industry Committee for National Advertising Readership Surveys.

washing machines and other consumer durables, whether they go to the cinema and other details. By analysing this information the advertiser can now answer the questions we posed above: how many people read each journal that has been bought, and who they are (i.e. are they likely to be prospective customers?). This data which provides the *readers per copy* and *demographic profile* of the 100 plus publications surveyed is, together with the ABC figures, the basic information used in *media planning*.

In the United States several market research companies produce readership surveys. Unfortunately the results produced by these surveys, which are often sponsored by individual media for their own promotional purposes, frequently conflict. This is because the questionnaires and research methods vary from one to another.

(ii) Regional newspapers. There are approximately 100 provincial daily newspapers in Britain and 1,200 weeklies. Together they carry £328,000,000 (1976) of advertising which makes them the biggest single advertising sector. However, much of the expenditure in the weeklies is attributable to local retail and local classified advertising. From the national advertisers' point of view, the most important of the provincial media are those published daily, the evening newspapers in particular. (This is because both the provincial morning newspapers and the local weeklies tend to have much smaller circulations and thus far fewer readers than the provincial evening papers.)

70% of all evening newspapers belong to an important institution called the Evening Newspaper Advertising Bureau (ENAB for short). ENAB works for all its members in three ways:

1. It promotes the use of advertising—particularly colour advertising—in local evening papers for national advertisers.
2. It co-ordinates the selling of certain advertising space, particularly classified through the *National Classified Advertising Service*.
3. Finally, it sponsors and publishes much useful market research into the readership of evening newspapers.

It is this last function which is of most significance to the national advertiser, who will frequently want to compare the cost-effectiveness of advertising either in say, national dailies or in a group of provincial evenings. This is the kind of data that ENAB publishes to help advertisers:

	Proportion of sales %	*Bristol Evening Post* Average No. of copies sold	No. of house-holds	% house-holds covered in area
Town of Publication				
Bristol	62·89	105,675	147,925	71·44
Districts				
Bristol	62·89	105,676	147,925	71·44
Kingswood	9·94	16,701	25,455	65·61
Northaron	9·19	15,449	32,627	47·35
Wansdyke	2·73	4,592	23,654	19·41
Woodspring	7·81	13,120	47,433	27·66
Remainder	7·44	12,505	—	—
Total	100·00	168,403	—	—

[Source: ENAB 1975]

Marketing Area Population (1971 Census)	821,491
No. of Households	277,093
Persons per Household	3
Adult Population—males	299,592
Adult Population—females	328,954
Owner-Occupied Households	155,367
Car-Owning Households	164,155

The publication by ENAB of this wealth of usable data has helped to give major advertisers confidence in the provincial evening newspapers as being well read, effective advertising media. And this, together with the growth in retailer advertising, has accounted for their considerable growth over recent years.

However, the *cost per thousand* circulation is usually higher in local papers than in the nationals. Compare for example the *Bristol Evening Post* with the *Sun*.

	Cost per S.C.C.	ABC Circulation	Cost per 1,000
Bristol Evening Post	£1·73	137,733	0·012p.
Sun	£20·50	3,738,765	0·005p.

[Source: BRAD (1976)]

Thus it is three times as expensive for an advertiser to reach a thousand buyers of the *Bristol Evening Post* than a thousand buyers of the *Sun*. For this reason national advertisers almost always use national newspapers *except* when there is a very specific reason for advertising in a locality.

(*iii*) *Consumer magazines.* There are over 1,000 consumer magazine titles published in the U.K. and they can be broadly divided into two groups:

> General interest and women's magazines
> Special interest and hobby magazines.

From the national advertisers' point of view, the first group is of greater importance than the second, but special interest and hobby magazines must always be remembered as an excellent way of reaching specific minority groups inexpensively.

The leading general interest and women's magazines have large circulations and thus considerable coverage of the population:

ABC Circulation (1976)

Woman	1,536,107
Woman's Own	1,557,834
Woman's Weekly	1,610,170
Readers' Digest	1,380,892
Tit-Bits	424,558
Reveille	549,027
Radio Times	3,614,730
TV Times	3,458,014
Punch	81,272

[Source: BRAD]

Moreover, because as we saw previously they lie around the house (and elsewhere) these magazines have more average *readers per copy* than newspapers do, so their readerships are far greater than their circulation figures suggest. *Punch* for example has an average of 14·7 readers per copy and thus a total readership of 867,000. This data comes from the comprehensive JICNARS National Readership Survey (1976).

At the end of this chapter you will find a chart summarising the advantages and disadvantages of all the different groups of media, from an advertiser's standpoint. But it is worth mentioning here that general interest and women's magazines are frequently interchangeable with the National press in their effectiveness as advertising media, and these two groups of publications are therefore highly competitive with one another.

This is not the case with special interest and hobby magazines, whose circulations (and advertising rates) are generally lower. On the next page are a few examples.

Some of the special interest and hobby magazines, mostly those with circulations of around 100,000 and upwards, are included within the JICNARS National Readership Survey —but the great majority are not. Additionally, many of the smaller circulation publications do not even subscribe to publish ABC figures. This means that advertisers must rely largely on their own judgement and experience as to whether a publication is likely to bring results, because so little concrete data is available.

ABC Circulation (1976)

Amateur Gardening	136,728
Amateur Photographer	73,915
Motor	78,541
Practical Householder	123,434
Melody Maker	153,709
Railway Magazine	53,054
Sewing and Knitting	99,113
Rugby World	23,400
Angling Times	175,483
The Connoisseur	17,541

[Source: BRAD]

Magazines do not usually sell advertising space by the single column centimetre, but by pages or fractions of a page i.e. ½ pages, ¼ pages and even smaller.

As with newspapers, the cost of space is roughly proportional to the size of circulation, but *special interest and hobby magazines* usually have a higher cost per thousand circulation than *general interest and women's magazines*.

All magazines charge more for colour and most charge more for advertisements *next to* or *facing* editorial matter. This is because it is believed that magazine readers are more likely to see an advertisement if it is close to the articles in the publication than if it is bunched in with a crowd of other advertisements, though there is no positive proof of this.

Here are examples of the costs of a standard whole page, black and white, in some of the magazines whose circulations have been noted above:

Basic rate, whole page black and white

Woman	£4,590	Amateur Gardening	£492
Readers' Digest	£3,030	Motor	£397
Reveille	£1,092	Railway Magazine	£120
Radio Times	£4,890	Rugby World	£132

[Source: BRAD (1976)]

(*iv*) *Trade and technical journals.* Trade and technical journals are, as we have seen, magazines that are published for people at their work. There are over 2,000 of them and compared with consumer magazines their circulations are quite small—the majority being well under 30,000. Probably fewer than 20% are affiliated to the Audit Bureau of Circulations, and none at all are included in the JICNARS National Readership Survey. However, several major publishing companies operate in the field of Trade and Technical Journals—including McGraw Hill, Morgan Grampian, Haymarket Press and IPC.

These companies produce for advertisers detailed information on the circulations of their magazines and who reads them. Almost all trade and technical journals are delivered by mail. You will rarely see any on sale at news stands. This means that the publishers can make a fairly accurate assessment of who reads them.

Additionally, under the control of the ABC, trade and technical journals are asked to supply a Media Data Form which gives details of their geographical distribution and of any readership breakdowns available. Much of this information, however, is based upon the magazine publishers' statements and therefore although it is normally highly reliable and accurate, it cannot be compared with the independently produced ABC circulation figures and JICNARS readership data.

Many of the journals are distributed free to their readers, and the publishers then rely on advertising revenue to cover the total cost of printing and distributing the magazine. It is a mark of the consistent effectiveness of such journals as advertising media that the publishers are able to do this.

Advertisement space in trade and technical journals is sold in much the same way as in consumer magazines—pages, $\frac{1}{2}$ pages, $\frac{1}{4}$ pages and so on, with premium prices for special positions next to editorial matter. Many larger magazines offer colour printing; most accept loose advertisement inserts, and many advertisers make use of this facility as it is a proven way of generating interest and direct response (if the advertiser is offering a brochure or other material).

Here are some examples of the circulations and advertising rates in trade and technical journals.

	Circulation	Basic Rate, whole page black and white
Works Management	24,313	£395
D-I-Y Trade	8,375	£165
Catering Times	12,275	£420
Office Equipment Index	54,990	£830
National Builder	16,028	£220
British Baker	9,491	£140

[Source: BRAD (1976)]

(v) *Directories* (*including Yellow Pages*). Though there are over 1,500 directories published in Britain this, as you will remember, is much the smallest segment of Press and Magazine advertising—less than 2% of the total. Directories are essentially vehicles for trade advertising. The best of them (the *Advertisers' Annual* is an excellent example) list every company operating in a particular trade or industry. Many trade directories, however, list only those companies willing to pay for an entry, in which case as directories they are not too useful. Such directories are becoming less fashionable and far fewer of them are published today.

In any event, entries in directories do not normally involve the skills of the advertising department, and much the same is true of Yellow Pages. The great majority of entries in Yellow Pages are those of small local traders and this medium is far less useful for national advertisers, particularly of consumer goods.

Excluding press production costs, which amount to a sizeable £53,000,000 (4·9% of the total) we have for the time being completed our analysis of the press and magazines as media for advertising. It is time now to explore television.

Television

Television advertising in the U.K. is strictly regulated by the government. Together with commercial radio, commercial television comes under the Independent Broadcasting Authority (IBA), and the IBA controls both the *volume* and the *content* of advertising. In this respect the broadcast media are unique. Although there are statutory controls on poster sitings, all the non-broadcast media are reasonably free to publish as much advertising as they wish, and the content of the advertisements is only controlled by certain general laws (particularly the Trades Description Act) and by a voluntary Code of Practice, self-imposed by the advertising industry. (We shall cover the controls of advertising in detail in Chapter 7.)

The consequences of the indirect governmental control of commercial television are considerable. First, the government has allowed only one commercial television network to operate in the U.K., so that this network has monopoly powers as far as advertisers are concerned (but not of course as far as viewers are concerned, since they have a choice of three stations to watch: ITV, BBC 1 or BBC 2). Secondly, the government decreed that commercial television, unlike the BBC, should be regional in nature; so the IBA has divided the country rather arbitrarily into thirteen regions and allocates contracts to commercial television companies region by region. Third, the government allows a maximum of 7 minutes advertising per hour, with the aim of avoiding what many people believe to be the excesses of television advertising in the U.S.A. and elsewhere. Fourth, the government insists that every commercial station must publish a *rate card* and that its advertising time *must* be sold at the rates detailed on the card, to minimise the possibilities of favouritism or corruption entering into the buying and selling of airtime.

Lastly, through the IBA the government vets all commercials both in script form and in their finished form to ensure

that they adhere to the IBA's strict regulations concerning
the content of commercials. (To which we shall return in
Chapter 7.)

Each of the commercial stations which cover the country
fixes its own rates for advertising time, and charges its
highest rates for that period of each day when most people
are watching television. This is called *peak time*. During peak
time between 25 %–40 % of the population with a television
set will be watching ITV. The station's rates are roughly
proportional to the size of the population in their region,
though some stations (particularly the London stations and
Southern) manage to charge a premium for their time
because demand for television advertising in the South-East
is somewhat stronger than in the rest of the country.

Here are the names of the commercial stations now
operating:

	Area	Homes covered (000's)	Cost of a 30 sec. peak time spot (1976)
Thames London Weekend } *	Greater London	4,330	{ £4,500
ATV	Midlands	3,020	£1,960
Anglia	East Anglia	1,120	£700
Granada	Lancashire	2,580	£1,650
Yorkshire	Yorkshire	2,010	£1,595
Tyne-Tees	North East	925	£685
Southern	South East	1,620	£780
Harlech	West & Wales	1,380	£780
Westward	South West	521	£378
Border	Scottish Border	185	£130
Scottish	Central Scotland	1,320	£592
Grampian	Highlands	210	£162
Ulster	Northern Ireland	397	£230

[Source: JICTAR and BRAD]

* Note that London has two programme stations. This is
because the IBA decided that no single station should have a
monopoly of this large and affluent market.

(Due to the positioning of transmitters, there is some overlap between certain regions, and people in these overlap areas can choose which commercial station they prefer to watch. This can cause problems for advertisers.)

Just as with JICNARS and the press, the audience for television is measured by market research sponsored by the entire advertising industry. This is called JICTAR, which stands for the Joint Industry Committee for Television Advertising Research.

JICTAR measures the audience for television in two ways:

1. It runs a sample panel of 2,655 homes, spread representatively over each of the thirteen regions. In each of these homes, with the owner's agreement the television set is fitted with a SET meter. This meter records continuously on to rolling tape whether the TV set is on or off, and if it is on, which station it is tuned to. From this data JICTAR can calculate, for example, how many homes throughout the country were watching television, and what they were watching, minute-by-minute on any occasion.

2. Additionally, in the same homes a member of the household keeps a TV viewing diary for the whole family and for guests. JICTAR can then say exactly how many people were watching the set when it was on, and whether they were adults or children, male or female.

All of the data is then returned by the households to a company called Audits of Great Britain Limited (AGB), one of the largest market research companies in Europe, who handle the JICTAR operation under contract. AGB process the data via a computer with great speed and publish a two-volume *Weekly TV Audience Report* within ten days after the week in question. These reports show on a minute-by-minute basis the percentage of sets tuned in to ITV, BBC 1 and BBC 2. This figure is the TV Rating. The reports thus show TV Ratings for all shows and commercials, in each region, approximately 10 days after their transmission.

The *television time buyer*, who is responsible for buying television advertising time for the advertiser, studies the TV Ratings carefully, and from them he predicts which programmes and which commercial breaks are likely to have the largest audiences in future. However, the television programme companies sell their time in broad segments (e.g. peak time lasts about 4 hours). If the time buyer wants to guarantee that his commercial will be transmitted during one particular break, he will probably need to pay an extra *fixing charge*, up to 15% of the cost of the spot. The time buyer will be aiming to achieve the lowest possible *cost per thousand* viewers, i.e. he will want as many viewers as possible to see his commercial at the least possible cost, in exactly the same way as the buyer of space in the press. Predicting the TV Ratings for each programme, deciding whether or not to pay fixing charges, choosing between expensive *peak time* and inexpensive *off-peak time* all combine to make television time-buying a highly specialised and skilful job—so that expert television time buyers are nowadays much sought-after and highly paid.

Posters and transport

The common denominator between *posters* and *transport* advertising is that both act outside the home and both generally must display simple, graphic advertising messages because they will be seen only briefly by people passing them. However, this rule does not apply to one sub-section of *transport* advertising: interior transport advertising—inside buses, trains and taxis—where the viewer often has time to read and absorb a much longer message.

Posters, usually called *billboards* in the United States, are subject to government legislation the aim of which is to control both the number and the placing of posters and to prevent them from disfiguring our towns and countryside. The *Town and Country Planning (Control of Advertisements) Regulations 1948* defined outdoor advertising as:

'any word, letter, model, sign, placard, board, notice, device or representation, whether illuminated or not, used for the purposes of advertisement, announcement or direction. It includes any hoarding or similar structure used or adopted for the display of advertisements. It also includes such forms of advertisement as a Doctor's nameplate.'

So you will see that every form of outdoor advertising from the neon light in Piccadilly Circus to your local doctor's sign come within the scope and control of the legislation.

1. Posters. The factors which define the strength of a poster campaign are:

(*a*) the number of posters put up (in any given area);
(*b*) the size of the posters;
(*c*) the specific siting of the posters;
(*d*) the length of the campaign.

(*a*) A reasonable *number* of posters for a campaign is usually judged to be ten sites per 100,000 population. Many more than this would constitute an above-average campaign, many fewer would probably be ineffective. A research study carried out in 1974 showed that a campaign of this weight

would be likely to be seen by 75% of the population
covered.

(*b*) Posters are available in standard sizes called 'sheet sizes'
which are based on the *double crown* size, 20 inches wide by
30 inches deep (50·8 cm × 76·2 cm). The most common
poster size you see is the 16-sheet (6 feet 8 inches × 10 feet)
(2·03 m × 3·00 m); larger sizes are 32-sheets and 48-sheets
which are twice and three times as wide respectively, but
the same depth.

The cost of a poster site is approximately proportional to
its size. The largest sizes are called *Bulletin Boards* (or
Supersites) which may be as long as 45 feet (137 m), and be
lit up. Bulletin Boards are usually hand-painted for the site,
whereas the great majority of the other posters are printed
on paper and pasted on to the site.

(*c*) Some poster sites are obviously better than others,
because they are in positions where more people will see
them. A poster at the end of a quiet suburban cul-de-sac
will be seen by far fewer people than one at a hectically busy
road junction. Some sites are better for reaching motorists
(those on major trunk roads for example), others are better
for reaching shoppers (like the smaller sites in pedestrian
precincts). Depending upon their requirements, advertisers
may either specify precisely which sites they want, which is
known as *line-by-line* buying, or alternatively they may buy a
Pre-Selected Campaign in which the poster company simply
supplies the best sites then available. Buying a *Pre-Selected
Campaign* is cheaper than buying *line-by-line*, but is not
always suitable.

(*d*) Many large companies, particularly cigarette and beer
companies, run their poster campaigns year-in year-out,
every month of the year. As a result these companies have
over the course of time acquired many of the best sites that
exist, and a new advertiser who wants these sites may find
that they are unavailable. Thus posters are not really the

best medium for short, intensive campaigns. Rather they must be used consistently, so that the advertiser can build up a selection of his own desired sites over the months and years. Finally, it is important to mention that, although posters are frequently thought of as a *support* medium, only to be used in conjunction with television or the press, many advertisers have used them on their own as a *solus* medium with great success. Moreover, posters are not an especially cheap medium. Precise costs depend upon sizes, sites etc., but an 'average' national campaign using sixteen sheets might cost as much as £500,000 in a full year.

2. Transport. Transport advertising is a less major medium than *posters*, being used to a large extent by local, smaller advertisers. The three main contractors for transport advertising are British Rail, National Bus Company and London Transport.

British Rail offer station sites (which like other posters can be bought in a group or individually), displays in trains and in BR ships and Hovercraft. The National Bus Company offers spaces on the sides, fronts and rears of the many local bus companies in Britain, together with interior sites which nowadays are sometimes illuminated.

Because of its size and importance as a market, and because of the London Underground system, national advertisers are perhaps more prone to advertise on London Transport than on the other two transport media. The underground is an especially effective way of inexpensively reaching London commuters, many of whom are young girls who represent a highly important market for clothes, cosmetics and entertainments.

Cinema

Cinema advertising is now used almost exclusively for reaching young audiences. This is because the growth of television has meant that older people stay at home more, and go to the cinema less and less. Here is a breakdown of the average cinema audience (1976):

	% Average Cinema Audience	% of total Population
Sex		
Male	57%	48%
Female	43%	52%
Age		
15–24	56%	18%
25–34	21%	18%
35+	23%	64%
Social Group		
AB	15%	12%
C1	26%	24%
C2	35%	32%
DE	26%	32%

[Source: JICNARS]

Despite this heavy bias towards the young, over half of the population under 45 years of age are still at least occasional cinemagoers, and the 1,500 or so cinemas in the United Kingdom receive over 140 million admissions each year. Therefore for certain advertisers, particularly those wishing to reach younger customers, the cinema remains a most influential medium.

As with television, cinema commercials are 15, 30, 45, 60 or even 90 or 120 seconds long. However, because almost nobody visits the same cinema to see the same film more than once in a week, cinemas sell their advertising time by the week. Larger cinemas charge more than smaller ones, and the cinemas in London's West End have their own, still higher rates. Again, because the number of people visiting a cinema in one week is comparatively small it is usual to run 6-week or 13-week campaigns—which increases both the number of people who see the advertising and the number of times that they see it. One week's campaign for a 30-second commercial in every cinema in the U.K. would cost approximately £9,000.

Radio

While commercial radio has long been established in the United States and elsewhere, in Britain it is much the youngest and newest of the advertising media.

As with television, commercial radio is a government-controlled advertising medium and the government has authorised nineteen stations throughout the country. The transmission areas for each station are given as an inner VHF area and an outer medium wave area. Taking the outer areas together, the nineteen stations can now reach a total of 30,000,000 adults—almost 75% of the adult population. However, audiences at any one time are quite small—Capital Radio in London, for example, reaches only 5% of adults in its area during its peak listening time of 8.00 a.m. to 8.30 a.m. on weekdays.

The percentage of people who listen to commercial radio at all also varies widely from station to station, as the following table shows:

Station	Area covered	Percentage of adults listening each week (1976)
London Broadcasting	London	19%
Capital	London	36%
Clyde	Glasgow	63%
BRMB	Birmingham	39%
Piccadilly	Manchester	36%
Metro	Newcastle	44%
Swansea	Swansea	63%
Hallam	Sheffield	45%
City	Liverpool	36%
Forth	Edinburgh	40%
Trent	Nottingham	42%
Plymouth	Plymouth	*Not yet available*
Tees	Stockton	41%
Pennine	Bradford	29%
Victory	Portsmouth	*Not yet available*
Orwell	Ipswich	*Not yet available*
Thames Valley	Reading	*Not yet available*
Downtown	Northern Ireland	*Not yet available*
Beacon	Wolverhampton	*Not yet available*

[Source: JICRAR]

Because the number of people listening at any one time is
so comparatively small, almost all advertisers buy time in
'packages'. Spot lengths are the same as for television—7, 15,
30, 45 and 60 seconds—and 60% of airtime is bought on the
basis of a 49-spot package (7 spots × 7 days weekly block).
This is generally recognised to be a medium weight campaign. It is, however, possible to buy on a specified spot-by-
spot basis, and to buy certain other packages—e.g. all at the
weekend, all in weekday day time—the costs of which vary
from station to station.

As always, advertising costs are approximately proportional to the number of people reached by each station. In
the case of radio this is dependent both on the *size* of the
population in the transmission area, and on the *percentage* of
the population regularly listening in. Here are the costs of
49-spot × 30-second packages on some of the stations:

Station	Cost of the 49-spot × 30-second package
Capital	£1,960
Clyde	833
Piccadilly	990
Plymouth	238
Orwell	226

[Source: BRAD (1976)]

It is possible to buy this 49-spot package on all nineteen
stations for approximately £10,000—less than a single
national peak-time spot on TV or a week's national cinema
campaign.

Research into radio listening is supervised by another
total advertising industry committee, the Joint Industry
Committee for Radio Advertising Research (JICRAR). As
the volume of expenditure on radio is much smaller than on
television or the press, it is not economically feasible to carry
out such sophisticated continuous research in this new
medium as in the other two. Instead JICRAR carries out
periodic surveys, using diaries, which the respondents themselves fill in, and publishes the results when they become
available.

When commercial radio first began in Britain, many people made the mistake of thinking of it as a national medium, like the BBC. Essentially, however, it is a local medium, more akin to local newspapers than to, say, the national press. This is reflected in the fact that 40% of the airtime is booked by local advertisers—though, predictably, by far the largest advertisers are record companies, and they alone provide about 20% of the stations' turnover.

Below-the-line

We have now completed our survey of the major advertising media. These are the media of mass-communication which carry the vast majority of all advertisements. They are usually described in advertising as the *prime media*; and they are the media where the expenditures listed at the beginning of this chapter are continuously measured and analysed.

However, there are many other forms of advertising, sometimes called *sales promotion*, sometimes *merchandising*, but most often *below-the-line* (because of the historic practice of many advertisers of dividing their budgets with a line between the mass-media described above, and other promotional activities). *Below-the-line* covers a vast range of sales techniques, and is increasingly being handled and organised by specialist companies set apart from advertising agencies. It is nevertheless essential for anyone in advertising to have a working knowledge of when, where and how below-the-line promotions should be used.

Generally, below-the-line promotions have a short-term or immediate impact on sales, while media advertising builds loyalty to a brand over the long-term. Moreover below-the-line promotions are more effective when backed up by strong, continuous brand advertising. For example free plastic daffodils are unlikely to persuade you to buy an unknown, unadvertised detergent called SPLURGE, while they were extremely effective in persuading millions and millions of housewives to buy heavily advertised DAZ.

Additionally, too frequent below-the-line promotions can be counter-productive in sales terms. Some years ago Ribena, the famous blackcurrant Vitamin C drink, virtually stopped all media advertising, in favour of regular below-the-line promotions with unfortunate results: first, supermarket buyers ceased to buy-in Ribena for their stores except when there was a promotion on offer. Second, housewives began to switch away from Ribena and buy other makes, particularly the less expensive (and usually less good) brands of the stores themselves. Ribena sales plummeted. Beecham, who own Ribena, quickly saw what was happening and re-started media advertising. The decline was halted, but Ribena sales have never fully recovered.

So with these provisos in mind, let us now look at the principal types of below-the-line promotion with a proven record of success as 'shot-in-the-arm' sales boosters when used *correctly*.

(*i*) *Giveaways*. These may be stuck on to the pack, put inside the pack, or mailed to the customer in return for labels or packet tops. They can be highly effective, though normally the giveaways must be very inexpensive items, since you cannot afford to give away a £20 gift with a packet of Kelloggs Corn Flakes! Giveaways in-pack are especially widely used for children's goods throughout Europe.

(*ii*) *Self-liquidating Premiums*. These are goods which the customer obtains at an especially low price in return for sending in money plus labels or packet tops. They are called 'self-liquidating' because the promotion does not actually cost the company anything. The company acquires the goods in bulk at a low price, and simply sells them at cost. They are generally less effective, in sales results, than giveaways.

(*iii*) *Prize competitions*. Again, these are not too effective nowadays, in sales terms, unless mounted on a very lavish scale and heavily advertised. It is best to have one extremely expensive, attractive first prize backed by many thousands of smaller prizes so that as many entrants as possible win something. Great care must be taken because the British laws concerning prize competitions are complex and strict: competitions must not rely purely on luck, there must be an element of skill.

(*iv*) *Gift coupons*. One of the oldest forms of promotion and highly effective in the right situation. Used extensively by retailers and petrol stations (Green Shield and Pink Stamps) and by cigarette brands. (Players No. 6 and Embassy, the two biggest sellers, both offer gift coupons.) But only really successful where the product or service is obtained sufficiently frequently for the coupons to build up reasonably quickly.

(*v*) *Cash vouchers*. Vouchers worth a cash sum—usually 5p or 10p—redeemable against the purchase of the product at a retailer. These are extremely useful for encouraging trial of a product, and therefore mostly used with new products. Distributed door-to-door, included in a newspaper advertisement or on another pack. Expensive, and the risk of mal-redemption (when the retailer accepts the voucher against the purchase of an entirely different product) is ever-present.

(*vi*) *Multi-packs*. Two or three packs banded together at a special reduced price. Can be extremely effective, especially for products where market research has shown that consumers frequently buy more than one pack at a time—petfoods, for example. Also useful for obtaining trial of new products, by banding them to popular established brands.

(*vii*) *Free samples*. Again expensive, but undoubtedly the best way of introducing a product to potential new users. Ideal for situations where market research has proved that consumers clearly perceive the product is superior to its competitors once they try it. (And extremely dangerous if the converse might be true!) Samples can be distributed door-to-door or in-store, possibly using a special personal demonstrator.

(*viii*) *Flash-packs and money-offs*. The original and still the best way to increase sales! But as was pointed out in the last chapter, it is easy to sell goods if you make the price low enough. Three dangers: (*a*) flash-packs can cheapen the appearance and quality of a brand; (*b*) repeated money-offs quickly lead to the Ribena situation described above and (*c*) they can work out highly expensive, because you are giving away money to customers who would have bought the brand anyway.

(*ix*) *Display and merchandising material*. This has become progressively less important in most consumer markets, as retailer chains either produce their own or specify exactly what they want and reject anything else. Nevertheless showcards, posters, hanging signs and dump bins (which contain packs of the product) are still well used. Truly inventive and unusual material will almost always be displayed.

(*x*) *Door-to-door distribution*. This is basically a medium of distribution for much of the promotional material detailed above. But it can of course also be used to distribute straightforward printed advertisements or sales literature. In this respect it is most frequently used by retailers to publicise locally their price-cuts and special promotions. Distribution costs work out at about £5–£10 per 1,000 (urban districts are obviously easier and cheaper to cover than rural ones).

(*xi*) *Mini-media*. Under this heading are included all those special, little advertising media which can be particularly apposite in the right circumstances: match boxes, promotional ballpens and other giveaways, theatre programmes, exhibitions, trade fairs, fêtes, aeroplane trailers (illegal over towns, but used at the seaside), balloons, T-shirts, sandwich-board men, and a host of others. When you work in advertising you will find that these easily get forgotten in the excitement of producing television commercials and large colour advertisements. But they are usually inexpensive and sometimes are perfect for a particular purpose.

Direct Mail

Direct mail advertising, through the post, is the final major media weapon in the advertiser's armoury. It is sometimes grouped together with below-the-line promotional activities, but for many types of advertiser it is their prime medium— even though it is not classed as one of the prime media for advertising as a whole.

As has previously been mentioned, direct mail is especially useful in industrial and technical marketing. Specialist direct mail companies hold lists of hundreds of thousands of individuals on computers, and the lists detail their full names, addresses and jobs. Because of the volume of direct mail publicity carried out by pharmaceutical companies and others within the medical sphere, for example, a company called Medical Mailing Limited has been able to operate highly successfully, providing lists of doctors, dentists, nurses and senior hospital staff to advertisers.

Since the 'irritation' factor in direct mail advertising is often commented upon, it is important also to mention its *informative* function. Advertising space in publications is generally too expensive for it to be possible (or desirable) for advertisers to cram their advertisements with information. (We have considered how dull and unreadable such advertisements look when discussing stock exchange prospectuses.) Direct mail literature, however, can be designed to be as long and as detailed as the advertiser wishes. This in turn will depend on what information the recipient requires. The extra cost of mailing a long, rather than a short missive is likely to be minimal. Hence industrial direct mail advertising often comprises detailed material that will be filed and used by the recipient, such as technical data sheets, and comprehensive informative leaflets printed to a standard size (usually A4).

While direct mail is primarily used as an effective advertising tool by industrial advertisers, it is, of course, also used extensively by some advertisers of consumer goods. It is frequently and successfully used by the publishers of expensive books—the *Readers' Digest* and Mitchell Beazley are masters of the art. Others who use it are companies who have built up lists of the names and addresses of people who have bought from them in the past and may therefore be likely to buy from them in future: seed companies, insurance, unit trust and holiday tour companies are all good examples of this. It is usually (though not invariably) the case that a previous customer is worth re-mailing three times. If the customer has not reordered after three attempts he has either moved, lost interest, or died!

The ownership of a good *list* can be a valuable asset for a company which has proved that it can generate sales via direct mail. Some seed companies, for example, obtain up to 20% of their business simply by mailing their new catalogue to their previous customers each year. Computerization has made the ownership and use of direct mail lists even more cost-effective, and it seems certain that despite rising postal costs this medium will grow in importance in Britain, as it already has done in the United States, where $3,920,000,000 was spent in 1974, just slightly less than was spent on U.S. television advertising in the same year.

Summary—Advantages and Disadvantages

It is not strictly possible to produce scientific generalisations about the differential effectiveness of the different advertising media. Many studies have attempted to do so, but too many variables enter the mix. How can you compare the *effect* of a 30-second commercial, a colour page in a women's weekly, and a direct mail shot, in a *generalised* way? Each will be better for specific purposes, worse for others. Many advertisers have discovered that while the sales of one product respond better to television, those of another respond better to national press. Here then is a charted summary of the known advantages and disadvantages of each of the media we have discussed. These will simply be the *main* factors that advertisers and their agencies consider before deciding where to spend their advertising budgets.

Media Group	Advantages	Disadvantages
Press		
National Newspapers	Extremely high circulations and readership. Low cost per thousand readers. Carry prestige. Quick and easy to book and cancel, i.e. flexible. Wide variety to choose from.	Little colour availability. Rather poor reproduction. No sound or movement.
Regional Newspapers	Ideal for local campaigns. Flexible *re* time. Inexpensive. Good for test markets.	More expensive costs per thousand than nationals. Little colour availability. Rather poor reproduction. Carry less prestige. No sound or movement.
Consumer Magazines	Great diversity to choose from. Most in colour, with good reproduction. Carry 'atmosphere' and editorial often relevant to products. Good for reaching 'minorities'.	Inflexible because of printing times. No sound or movement. Small circulation magazines have expensive cost per thousand.
Trade and Technical Publications	Ideal for industrial advertisers. Good reproduction, colour available. Carry editorial relevant to products. Highly specific for target markets.	Slightly inflexible *re* time. Carry little prestige. Small circulations may miss important prospects. No sound or movement.
Directories (incl. Yellow Pages)	Useful as works of reference.	Not really effective as 'advertising' media for consumer advertising.
Television	Sound and movement. Extremely high coverage. Colour	Very expensive. Not very flexible *re* time. Still black and white

Media Group	Advantages	Disadvantages
Television—(*contd.*)	now reaches almost 50% of population. Proved to generate national and/or regional. Good for test markets. Highly 'emotionally involving'.	for 50% of population. Not seen at all by almost 10%. AB classes and teenagers are light viewers. Monopoly situation makes time buying difficult.
Posters and Transport	Colour and impact. High coverage/visibility. Close to shops and points-of-purchase. On display 24 hours per day. Flexible national and/or local. Can be pinpointed locally.	Poor flexibility *re* time. Usually 'slow-acting' in terms of generating sales.
Cinema	Ideal for younger audiences. Flexible national and/or local. Colour, sound and movement. Can achieve audience involvement.	Poor coverage of adults. Advertisements seen in 'group' situation. Difficult to achieve repetition of advertising message. Somewhat inflexible *re* time.
Radio	Inexpensive. Ideal for local campaigns. Flexible *re* time. Cheap to produce commercials.	High frequency of repetition needed. Somewhat low coverage. Not yet a national medium. No colour (or movement).
Below-the-line	Great diversity of possibilities. Fast sales generation. Generally inexpensive. Influential with retail trade. Generally flexible *re* time.	Dangerous if used too much. No possibility of building brand image and loyalty. May harm 'quality' of product.
Direct Mail	Excellent for industrial advertisers. Can be detailed and informative. Personalised. Good for consumer advertisers with effective lists. Very flexible *re* time. Production quality totally under control. Can be tested inexpensively.	Mass mailings very expensive. Mis-addressing highly wasteful. Suitable for few consumer products.

Think Exercises

1. 'In life you always gets what you pays for', said the tough old client, 'and if a 30-second peak-time spot on TV costs just about the same as 4 whole pages in *Woman*, you can take it from me they'll be just about equally effective.' Advance all the arguments you can think of to convince him the situation is not quite as straightforward as that.

2. Think of half a dozen useful advertising mini-media not included in the list on page 90.

3. Try to dream up a special interest magazine which will appeal to a sizeable section of the population but which, so far as you know, does not currently exist. Give it a title and outline the area the contents would cover. Then consider what kind of company would be especially likely to advertise in it? Are there likely to be enough advertisers to make it a reasonable commercial proposition?

4

The 3-Way Structure of the Advertising Industry: The Agencies

When most people think about advertising, they automatically think about advertising agencies. Advertising agencies seem to glow with glamour and excitement. Those outside advertising enjoy a stereotype vision of agencies housed in sleek modern offices, peopled with smooth grey-flannel-suited executives and chic, beautiful secretaries. They know that agencies are the places where 'adverts get dreamed up' and vaguely feel that agencies are the core of the advertising process.

On almost all counts the reverse is true. There are more people employed in the advertising departments of the media and of manufacturers than in advertising agencies themselves. While agencies no doubt have their share of smooth executives and chic secretaries, most agency people these days are ordinary, hardworking business people and office workers; and because of the exorbitantly high rents in central London, there has been a drift of agencies away from the central West End towards less romantic Paddington, Victoria and Camden Town. (In the United States there has similarly been a drift away from Manhattan, and agencies nowadays thrive throughout the country.) Finally, as by now you no doubt realise, the really crucial links in the advertising chain are the advertisers—who pay for it all—and the media—which carry the advertisements to the customers. What then, exactly, are advertising agencies? And how has it come about that they are so identified with the whole of the advertising process in the public mind?

History

The first advertising agents appeared in London at the beginning of the nineteenth century. Around that time the newspapers began to realise how much revenue they could raise if they set about selling their advertising space professionally. To do this they employed sales agents in rather the same way that insurance companies employ brokers; and they paid the agents a commission on sales, again in much the same way as insurance companies. At that time the commission for advertising agents was frequently as much as 25%.

During the course of the nineteenth century, and particularly in the United States, the role of the advertising agent changed, though not completely. Agents came to realise that although they were paid their commission by the newspapers, without the advertisers there would be no commission for them to earn. Moreover, certain agents built up exceptionally good businesses by acting as trusted advisors to advertisers. They counselled their clients on which were the best newspapers to buy space in, and steered them away from newspapers with untruthfully inflated circulations or inordinately high advertising rates. Thus agents developed divided loyalties: on the one hand to the media who paid them their commission, on the other hand to the advertisers who kept them in business. Once again the comparison with brokers is apt. Good professional brokers get their commissions from the insurance companies but give their customers the best possible advice on their policies. That, however, is as far as the analogy goes, close as the resemblance is.

During the course of the nineteenth century two fundamental developments took place which transformed agencies into the particular structures that they are today. First, and this appears very much to have started in America, agents began to offer clients extra services: they started to write and design the advertisements, free of charge. At first this was an area of competition between agents: some created advertisements, others did not. However, quite soon no advertiser was willing to use any agent who was not prepared to produce advertisements for him. As a result agencies became specialists and experts in the creation of advertisements. And they competed among themselves for clients by aiming to be better than each other at creating effective advertising.

This development was very much in the interest of the newspapers as clearly they have a vested interest in the success of advertisements: advertisers who are successful spend more on advertising. The greater the incentive among agencies to produce more effective advertising, the more the newspapers liked it. This brought about the second fundamental development. Realising that it was in their interests, newspapers gradually proceeded to rationalise and organise the agency business. This rationalisation had four basic components:

1. Newspapers agreed to pay the same commission to recognised agents—namely 15%.
2. *Only* recognised agents would be paid commission, and they would not be permitted to rebate any part of the commission to their advertiser clients.
3. To obtain recognition agents would need to apply to the newspapers and prove their financial probity and reliability, because . . .
4. Although called 'agents', they would legally become 'principals', responsible for paying for advertising space booked by them on their clients' behalf—even if the clients defaulted.

These four conditions still apply in Britain and have been adopted not only by newspapers but also by magazines, television, radio and cinemas. They apply too throughout most of the world—though in the United States the Federal Trade Commission has ruled that the non-rebating of commission is a restraint on competition and therefore it has been dropped.

There are perhaps 600 advertising agencies in the U.K. today (1977), employing approximately 14,000 people. (Over recent years the number of people employed has dropped quite considerably from 20,000 at the end of the 1960s.) Many of these agencies are very small—almost literally one-man-bands—but the largest 300 account for well over 90% of all advertising placed.

In the United States there are estimated to be approximately 4,000 agencies employing some 70,000 people; and these figures have been reasonably stable for some years.

The Functions of Agencies

As a consequence of their origins, agencies today serve both media and advertisers, in the following ways:

Agencies' Services to the Media:

(*a*) Agencies prepare professional, effective advertisements which generally enhance the appearance of the media in which they appear.

(*b*) They ensure that the advertisements arrive at the media in the technically correct state for reproduction or transmission. (Imagine an advertiser who was also an enthusiastic amateur cinematographer cutting together his own film for a commercial. The likelihood is that it would be technically quite unsuitable for TV transmission.)

(*c*) They ensure that the advertisements arrive at the media on time.

(*d*) They act as a 'pressure group' for the sale of more advertising space and time.

(*e*) They collect the debts for space and time from the advertisers they work for, and pay the media promptly. (If agencies do not pay the media in the month following the appearance of an advertisement, they are liable to be charged heavy interest rates and/or lose their 15% commission.)

(*f*) Finally, as has already been stated, when they book space they act as principals-at-law and so must pay for the space even if they do not get paid themselves. In 1975 agencies had to pay approximately £1,000,000 to the media on behalf of defaulting clients. This system absolves the media from checking the financial reliability of the 50,000 or so advertisers whom the 600 agencies serve.

These are all strong reasons why the media believe it still to be greatly in their own interests to pay the agencies their 15% commission on space and time booked. However, as anyone who works in an advertising agency will tell you, most of their day-to-day work is in the service of the advertiser; and it is for their services to advertisers that agencies are most necessary.

Because of the commission system advertisers obtain these services, in a sense, free of charge. (Though of course the advertiser is paying for all the advertising out of which the media pay the agencies.) Also, because all agencies are paid the same 15%, and are not allowed by the media to rebate any of this commission, there is virtually no price competition in the agency business. (This is what the FTC objected to in the United States.) The lack of price competition has resulted, as it always does, in competition of other kinds. Agencies compete fiercely among themselves by offering either *more* services or *better* services (or ideally *more* and *better* services!).

Thus when we come to specify the services agencies provide for advertisers, it is necessary to preface the list by saying that not all agencies provide all the services listed; that not all advertisers require the same services from their agency; and that sometimes the services may be provided by the agency free (i.e. within their 15% commission) whereas in other instances—particularly for smaller clients—the agency may make supplementary charges. (The media merely rule that 15% is the *least* agencies may charge; about 25%–30% of agencies' total revenue comes from additional fees separate from commissions.)

This complex situation has developed over the last decade, particularly in the United States. Both there and in the U.K. specialist companies have grown up which now carry out certain of the jobs previously carried out by agencies. How far this trend will go is uncertain. Some people believe that *all* the functions currently performed by agencies could be more efficiently performed by smaller, totally specialised organisations. In the United States the FTC ruling mentioned above gave extra impetus to the split-up of agency services into smaller units. It is argued in favour of this development that it allows advertisers to shop around and buy the particular services that they require, without paying (via the commission system) for those that they do not want. However, this argument ignores the role of agencies *vis-à-vis* the media, and minimises too the great advantages an advertiser obtains from getting his total advertising plans co-ordinated and produced under one roof. Unquestionably at this moment the vast majority of advertisers, in the United States and certainly in Britain, prefer to use the services of a complete agency, and have made clear that they intend to continue doing so.

This may all sound rather complicated, but will become clearer when we now look in detail at the services involved:

Agencies' services to their advertiser clients:
(*a*) Agencies advise clients upon which media to advertise

in, and seek to buy space and time for their clients at the lowest possible cost. This is one of the basic, historic functions of an agency which applies almost universally in agency–client relationships.

(*b*) Agencies create and produce for their clients the advertisements which appear in the media. This too is an absolutely basic, almost universal function.

(*c*) Agencies advise clients on their total marketing and sales operation, as experienced and independent outsiders. This may not always be formalised—it may simply occur at lunch or over a drink—but again it occurs very widely.

(*d*) Agencies test and research the advertisements they create, and analyse the results of campaigns that have been run. There is usually, but not always, a supplementary fee for advertisement testing; campaign result analysis, when it can be done, is free.

(*e*) Agencies carry out package designs and get closely involved in new product development. This is by no means universal, and agencies almost always charge supplementary fees for these services. Some advertisers prefer to employ small, specialist companies for package design and new product development; others prefer to do the work 'in-house' within their own organisation.

(*f*) Agencies generate and carry out below-the-line promotional ideas for their clients. Again this is not a universal practice and agencies usually charge supplementary fees for such work. There are now many specialist companies working in this area, with greater experience and know-how than agencies often have.

(*g*) Agencies supervise, and sometimes carry out, market research for their clients. This practice was widely prevalent in the 1950s and early 1960s, but today the great majority of major advertisers carry out their own market research—discussing it with their agencies, of course, but commissioning it themselves from market

research companies. Again supplementary fees are
payable when the agencies do the work.

(*h*) Agencies sometimes own public relations subsidiaries;
other agencies have public relations departments within
their organisations. As with market research, however,
the practice of advertising agencies being responsible for
public relations was far more prevalent 15–20 years ago
than it is today.

Services (*a*), (*b*), (*c*) and (*d*) are today the most vital
agency functions. Those listed (*e*) to (*h*) are peripheral to the
agency's basic work, even though most agencies greatly
enjoy getting involved in them, and sometimes make useful
profits out of them (though almost equally often they make
losses by incurring costs far in excess of the fees they charge!).

All of this should not be surprising to you, if you remember our fundamental definition of an advertisement at the
beginning of Chapter 1. The creation, production and
placing of advertisements is, nowadays, what the advertising
agency business is primarily about.

Types of agency

From the foregoing it will already have become apparent to
you that the 600 agencies in Britain are not all exactly the
same as each other. And in the United States the diversity of
agency organisation is, if anything, even greater. However—
agencies are now to be found in virtually every country in
the world—even in Communist bloc countries—and though
their organisations may vary, their basic functions are
always the same.

An advertiser thinking of appointing a new agency will
need to choose one that is precisely right for his type of
business. The appointment of the right advertising agency is
an extremely important decision for an advertiser; if he
chooses one that is unsuitable then the agency–client relationship will almost certainly be unsatisfactory, inefficient
and short-lived. The best agency to handle Coca-Cola's

multi-million pound advertising budget is most unlikely to be the best agency for a small rubber grommet manufacturer spending a few thousand pounds each year; and vice versa.

The different types of agency can be classified in three ways:

1. By the kind of advertising usually handled;
2. By size;
3. By locality.

Let us examine each of these in turn.

1. Kind of advertising handled. Owing to the diverse nature of advertising, and to the varying services that different advertisers require, many agencies now specialise in handling particular kinds of advertising. The main divisions are:

(*i*) International and full-service agencies;
(*ii*) Packaged-goods agencies;
(*iii*) Industrial agencies;
(*iv*) Specialist agencies: financial, recruitment, retailer, direct response and pharmaceutical.

We shall now consider how different agencies go about specialising in these different areas. However, it is important to emphasise beforehand that agency specialisation is rarely absolute: many *industrial* agencies will have one or two *packaged-goods* accounts, most agencies occasionally produce *financial* or *recruitment* advertisements for their clients if the circumstances so demand. This is akin to a plumber occasionally doing some building work or a builder doing some plumbing. Nevertheless most agencies decide upon how far they want to specialise and what area they aim to specialise in and then try to build their business within the areas they have chosen.

(*i*) *International and 'full-service' agencies.* By no means all 'full-service' agencies are international, though most now are; and not all international agencies are 'full-service', though the great majority are. However, it is necessary to group international and 'full-service' agencies together because of the degree of overlap between them, and because all of these agencies tend *to specialise in being non-specialist*. That is the basic meaning of 'full-service': it means that the agency is large enough to employ specialist departments which can handle every kind (or almost every kind) of advertising *within its own organisation*. Most international agencies fall into this category because, firstly, the international agencies tend to be the larger ones; and secondly because if they are serving a client in many countries around the globe it usually makes economic sense for them to handle the totality of his business rather than merely a part of it.

Sometimes the largest 'full-service' agencies hive-off their specialist departments into separate, but wholly owned, subsidiaries. Thus J. Walter Thompson, still the largest single agency in the world, owns a large pharmaceutical specialist subsidiary called Deltakos; and Leo Burnett, another of the world's top ten agencies, owns the specialist Leo Burnett Recruitment Agency. But these situations are comparatively exceptional. Generally speaking, 'full-service' agencies say to their own and to prospective clients: 'Whatever kind of advertising you require, we will produce it for you—so long as we can make a reasonable profit doing so.'

In Chapter 8 we will return to a detailed analysis of the functions, problems and opportunities involved in international advertising, which international agencies must be geared to handle. However, it is worth noting here that all of the very largest advertising agencies in Britain are international 'full-service' agencies, and that out of the top ten, nine are American-owned. Here is a list of them:*

>Masius, Wynne-Williams
>J. Walter Thompson
>Ogilvy Benson & Mather
>McCann-Erickson

* Source: Media Expenditure and Analysis, 1976.

Saatchi & Saatchi Garland-Compton
Young & Rubicam
Ted Bates
Leo Burnett
Davidson Pearce Berry & Spottiswoode
* Collett Dickenson & Pearce

(ii) Packaged-goods agencies. Traditionally, and especially
before the recent massive growth in retailer advertising, the
great majority of the largest advertisers throughout the
world were the manufacturers of branded packaged goods.
Such manufacturers discovered, as we saw in Chapter 2,
that they need to spend heavily and consistently over the
years to keep the sales of their products at high and increasing levels. They typically use television advertising or large
spaces in the press and women's magazines. And their products are frequently not greatly different from those of their
competitors, so producing their advertising calls for a considerable degree of creative ingenuity and brilliance.

Because the advertising budgets for branded packaged
goods tend to be large, and the media used tend to be
expensive, agencies specialising in this area usually employ
fewer staff than other types of agency of similar size; they
are particularly able to economise in their administrative
and clerical departments. On the other hand they have to
pay especially high salaries to their creative employees in
order to ensure that they can get and hold the finest and
most original advertising talent available.

(iii) Industrial agencies. Agencies specialising in industrial or
trade and technical advertising by contrast find themselves
working for clients with much smaller advertising budgets,
and have to place many more advertisements in comparatively inexpensive media. Remember that agencies get
paid 15 % commission on the media cost of each advertisement they book, and you will immediately see that this
must have a profound effect on their economic position.

* British-owned.

For example, if a packaged-goods agency produces one commercial which runs twenty times on national television, the media cost will be approximately £200,000. Whereas if an industrial agency produces an advertisement which runs twenty times in, for example, *National Builder* the total cost will be only £3,000. A comparison of the agencies' income from each of these campaigns shows:

$$\text{Television campaign: } 15\% \times £200,000 = £30,000$$
$$\text{Industrial campaign: } 15\% \times £3,000 = £450$$

This comparison is an extreme one; but the basic situation is typical, and leads to four consequences:

1. For the same volume of billings industrial agencies need to employ far more staff than other types of agency;
2. Industrial agencies almost always need to charge their clients service fees in addition to their media commissions;
3. Industrial agencies tend to pay their staff, particularly creative staff, rather lower salaries than other types of agency;
4. Industrial agencies tend to make rather smaller profits, as a percentage of billings, than other types of agency.

If all this makes life in an industrial agency sound rather gloomy, it must be pointed out that there are positive compensating advantages.

Industrial advertising, while intricate and complex, can also be extremely rewarding. As was made clear in Chapter 2, its value to commerce and to society cannot be in question. The products being advertised can generally be seen to be of direct benefit to industry and to the economy. Moreover life in industrial agencies is rarely as competitive or as frenetic as in packaged-goods agencies, where the high stakes sometimes lead to excesses and to strain.

(iv) Specialist agencies. Certain agencies have specialised narrowly in particular types of advertising. The main areas for such specialization are:

Financial
Recruitment
Retailer
Direct response
Pharmaceutical

In each of these areas there are up to about twenty small,
specialist agencies. Some of these, as has already been
pointed out, are subsidiaries of much larger 'full-service'
agencies. Others are wholly independent, usually owned by
one or two principals who have a special interest in and
knowledge of the subject and its advertising.

The reasons why some agencies have found it worthwhile
specialising in these limited areas apply to them all:

(*a*) In many cases specialist legal knowledge is called for—
     particularly for financial, direct response and pharma-
     ceutical advertising.
(*b*) In many cases advertising needs to be produced very
     speedily and flexibly—particularly for financial, recruit-
     ment, retailer and direct response advertising.
(*c*) In certain cases specific technical and/or scientific
     knowledge is required—particularly for financial and
     pharmaceutical advertising.
(*d*) In certain cases detailed experience of the effectiveness
     of different media is called for—particularly for finan-
     cial, recruitment and pharmaceutical advertising.

For all of these reasons some clients operating in each of
these areas prefer to appoint and work with specialist
agencies. However, there are also other clients who argue
that such specialisation inevitably fetters an agency's creativity, and these clients believe that they will be better served
by appointing non-specialist 'full-service' agencies and
gaining the benefit of their wider experience across the total
spectrum of advertising problems.

As with industrial agencies, of which they are in some
respect a sub-division, specialist agencies usually have a

higher-than-average ratio of staff to billings and frequently find it necessary to charge their clients fees additional to their 15% commission income.

2. Agency size. Agency size is the second main way of classifying agencies. As with the divisions between types of agency described above, the boundary lines between different sizes of agency are not hard and fast. Nor could they ever be, because agencies can grow rapidly, doubling or trebling in size in one successful year, just as they can shrink rapidly when things are not going well. Nevertheless, when a client is appointing a new agency, its present size and its likely growth over the next few years will be of the utmost importance to him. Agencies may be simply divided into three broad size groups:

> *Small:* Billing less than £2,000,000 and employing up to 30 people;
> *Medium:* Billing £2,000,000–£7,000,000 and employing 30–120 people;
> *Large:* Billing over £7,000,000 and employing more than 120 people.

Normally a client will wish to have an agency working for him that is neither too big, nor too small adequately to handle his account. If the agency is too big, then as a small customer he may suffer by being a little neglected when the agency is busy; agencies, like any other commercial organisation, will invariably ensure that their biggest and most important clients are served first and fastest on those occasions when not everybody can be served at once. If, on the other hand, the agency is really too small then it may not be able to offer the wide range of services that his account ought to command—and, perhaps more seriously, the agency is likely to lose a degree of its independence of spirit for fear of losing the account.

This leads to one other important aspect of agency size, the *breakdown of its accounts.* Three agencies may all be billing say £3,000,000 but their breakdown of accounts may be quite different, thus:

	Agency A	*Agency B*	*Agency C*
No. of accounts billing over £1,000,000	1	nil	nil
No. of accounts billing £500,000–£1,000,000	nil	2	nil
No. of accounts billing £250,000–£500,000	1	3	1
No. of accounts billing £100,000–£250,000	7	5	11
No. of accounts billing less than £100,000	11	7	27

It will be seen that Agency A is dominated by a single very large account, whereas Agency C has a raft of smallish accounts with almost no representation in the 'big league'. Agency B's breakdown of accounts, however, is an almost perfect 'pyramid' in which no single client is overwhelmingly preponderant but all seventeen clients are significant to its total turnover. Which of the three agencies a prospective new client will appoint will partly depend (among many other factors) upon the size of his own advertising appropriation. If his appropriation is worth about £1,000,000 he may prefer to go to agency A, which has a proven capacity to handle accounts of that size; if his account is worth £500,000 he should prefer to go to B, rather than to A where their one big account will still be dominant, or to C where he, in turn, may be dominant; if his account bills only £30,000 he will probably be best served by C, whose expertise lies in handling accounts of that size.

Finally, in discussing this important matter of agency size, it is essential to add that clients by no means always behave rationally, and some huge advertisers delight in being the biggest fish in a small pool; whereas some minuscule advertisers can only feel confident if they have employed one of the largest agencies in the world!

3. Locality. The third main classification of agencies is by locality, the principle division being between agencies in

London and those in the provinces. London, as most people know, is the centre of the advertising agency business in Britain (just as New York is the centre in the United States). But nevertheless much agency activity goes on outside London, and approximately 4,000 of the 14,000 people employed in agencies work in the provinces, especially in Manchester and Glasgow. (Likewise in the United States there are agencies scattered throughout the nation, with concentrations in Chicago and Los Angeles.)

As with specialist agencies, some provincial agencies are the subsidiaries of large London agencies. But most of them are independent operations, owned by their principals. None of them are really large, the biggest being an agency named Cogent Elliott at Solihull near Coventry which has billings approaching £5,000,000. Provincial agencies exist primarily to serve local advertisers who do not feel the need for an agency in the metropolis. Such advertisers are almost always small ones, and much of the business handled by provincial agencies is either for local industrial companies or for local retailers. However, certain national advertisers also believe that they can obtain better service and better advertising by employing out-of-London agencies. Such agencies' overhead costs are lower, and their finger-tips may be closer to the real pulse of the nation than are those of sophisticated, intellectual admen living in Hampstead or Chelsea.

These feelings are, perhaps not surprisingly, especially common among clients in Scotland. In consequence both Glasgow and Edinburgh have thriving groups of successful agencies, working for Scottish clients and frequently producing outstandingly effective and professional advertising.

Agency structure and organisation

At first sight it may seem surprising that we have left the discussion of agency structure and organisation until so late in this chapter. This has been done for two reasons. First, it

is far easier to understand the structure of an organisation if
you understand the purpose that structure is designed to
serve. Second, as you will by now have realised, just as
agencies vary widely in size, type and specialisation, so their
structures vary widely, reflecting the kind and style of the
business they handle.

Clearly tiny agencies, one-man-bands, will not have
complex organisational structures. Nevertheless, all agencies
require six basic departments; even if a single person carries
out the functions of four or five departments himself!
Those basic departments are:-

> (*i*) Management
> (*ii*) Client service
> (*iii*) Creative
> (*iv*) Media
> (*v*) Traffic and production
> (*vi*) Finance and book-keeping

Additionally, larger agencies will often include within their
organisation these eight extra departments:

> (*vii*) Television production
> (*viii*) Merchandising and promotion
> (*ix*) Marketing
> (*x*) Market research
> (*xi*) Personnel
> (*xii*) International
> (*xiii*) Public relations
> (*xiv*) Conferences and exhibitions

Let us look at the functions of each of these departments in
turn and then at the end consider how they interlock and
work together.

(*i*) *Management*
All organisations, of course, need management and direction. In advertising agencies the overall management is

normally vested in the board of directors, one of whom will be managing director and principally responsible.

The other directors will almost always have departmental and executive responsibilities in addition to their directorial ones, i.e. one director will be in charge of the creative department, another in charge of the media department, another of the finance department and several will be in charge of the handling of individual clients.

The frequency of the directors' or management meetings will vary, but will normally not be more often than weekly nor less than monthly. In the largest agencies, the directors frequently appoint a small sub-committee to be responsible for agency management to avoid the necessity for too frequent gatherings of the full board.

(ii) Client Service

To make it simple for their clients to deal with them efficiently, all agencies nominate specific individuals to be responsible for the handling of each account. At the most senior level a board director will have overall responsibility for the account, and he will be backed up by one or more client service executives, with varying levels of seniority and experience depending upon the specific requirements of each individual client. The job titles given to these executives also vary from agency to agency, but the most senior are usually called account director, account supervisor or account manager; and these are aided by account executives, account representatives or account co-ordinators.

'Co-ordination' is indeed the key word in all client service executives' job specifications. Client service people must co-ordinate their clients' needs with the agency's output, making sure that the right work gets done when the client wants it, if not before. They must also co-ordinate all the agency's own departments in the service of their client, ensuring that the creative department, for example, write and design advertisements which will fit the spaces the media department has booked. This may sound like routine, mechanical work but this co-ordination is, in fact, all too likely to breakdown in the hustle and bustle of agency life unless tremendous care and attention is paid to it.

The basic documentation used by client service executives to achieve accurate co-ordination is the *contact report*. Contact reports are effectively minutes of all the agency's meetings and telephone conversations with clients. They must be produced by the client service executive as soon as possible after any contact with the clients, certainly no later than 48 hours afterwards. The *contact report* will detail all decisions and agreements arrived at during the meeting with the client, and a copy of the contact report will be sent to the client as confirmation. Simultaneously other copies of the report will be distributed to all relevant people throughout the agency, to inform them of what is happening on the account and what action needs to be taken.

Client service executives are the agency's representatives at most meetings with clients. They therefore need to be clear-thinking, articulate, confident, likeable, hard-working, and above all capable of listening to and understanding a client's problems, and convincing the client that the agency's solution to those problems, when it has been produced, is the right one.

(iii) Creative

The creative department of an advertising agency can be compared to the shop floor in a factory. It is here that the goods (advertisements) are produced by which, in the end, the factory (agency) stands or falls. The creative department first produces the basic concept of all new advertisements. Then it produces the words (*copy*), the design (*layout* and *typography*) and, together with outside specialists, produces the actual photographs, drawings or film which will finally appear in the media.

The creation of advertisements bears no resemblance to the creation of pure art. Advertisements cannot be produced in a vacuum. Advertisements, as we have seen, are always produced for a specific purpose, usually to help in selling. The artists and writers who work in agency creative departments must be not merely inventive and original but also highly disciplined. They must accept and understand the brief they receive from the client, usually via a client

service executive. Then they must create a clear, comprehensible and relevant advertising answer to this brief. Needless to say this is extremely difficult and demanding work, which is why the best and most talented agency creative people get paid exceptionally highly.

(iv) Media

As its name implies, the media department is responsible for the agency's contact with all the different media. The department's function can be split into two parts: planning and buying. The planning function comprises analysing all the possible media available for a client's campaign, calculating the costs per thousand and other relevant figures, and then recommending to the client a media plan.

After discussion, when the plan has been amended if necessary and agreed by the client, it is the media department's job to carry out the buying of the space and time at the lowest possible cost. This calls for wheeling, dealing and negotiating skills of a high order. Because the skills called for in a successful *buyer* are not the same as the skills needed to be a successful *planner*, these two functions are often separated within agency media departments. Recently, however, this practice has come into question, since a good planner needs to know which media are 'soft' and can be bought cheaply, and which cannot; and a good buyer needs to know how essential it is that one medium should be used rather than another in order to play off competing media against each other and thus get the best possible bargains for his agency's client.

(v) Traffic and Production

The traffic and production functions within an agency are actually quite distinct, but today are usually to be found integrated in one department. Traffic (sometimes called *progress*) is the department responsible for overseeing and controlling the flow of work through the agency—and particularly through the creative department.

Following a client briefing, the client service executive will normally open a *job requisition*. This *job requisition* is a numbered card with four or five carbon copy sheets attached to it.

On the *job requisition* card will be typed details of the work required:

> The brief;
> Where and when the advertising is likely to appear;
> Specification details (size, printing process etc.);
> Dates when the work is needed by the client;
> Any other significant information.

The card will then be given to the traffic department, whose duty it will be to ensure that the work gets done as specified. One carbon of the *job requisition* will go to the media department, one to finance, one to production (if production is a separate department), one possibly to the client, and one will be kept by the client service executive. In this way all relevant departments within the agency will be kept informed of details of the jobs in hand.

The traffic department having progressed and chased the work through the agency, the job will finally end up in the *production* department. In an agency the production department is not what its name implies, since it is the creative department that is really responsible for *producing* the agency's output. The production department is so-called because it interlocks with the production departments in the media: the departments which actually print and produce the newspapers and magazines. The agency production department liaises with media production departments and ensures that the agency's advertisements are sent to them in the technically correct form for reproduction. (This subject will be covered in part (*viii*) of the next chapter.)

The reasons why traffic and production are nowadays frequently (but not universally) integrated into one department are partly technical—the result of photosetting and artwork being used more extensively for reproduction, in place of metal type and metal printing blocks; and partly the result of a realisation by agency management that the knowledge and skills required to do the jobs efficiently are much the same in both cases.

(*vi*) Finance and bookkeeping

The finance (or *accounts*) department of an advertising agency, like any other finance department, is primarily responsible for collecting money quickly from debtors—principally the agency's clients—and paying creditors—principally the media. It will also be responsible for the financial forecasting, cost controls, paying wages and

salaries, producing the company's annual accounts, liaising
with the inland revenue on tax matters, and keeping a tight
rein on petty cash!

The major financial problem facing an agency is that of
cash flow. As we saw earlier in the chapter, one of the key
components in an agency's relations with the media is that
it must pay them promptly in order to get paid its commission. The television companies and the major national newspapers and magazines are especially strict about this,
demanding payment by the 25th day of the month following
the date the advertisement appears. Unfortunately not all
clients are prompt payers, and therefore despite their most
stringent efforts, agencies quite often find themselves forced
to pay the media before they have been paid themselves. If
you calculate that a small agency with billings of only say
£1,000,000 has an average monthly turnover of over
£80,000, you will see that this problem can cause an agency
acute financial trouble if allowed to get out of control.
Most agencies therefore, especially young ones, need to
arrange a good overdraft facility with their bank.

The other important and difficult financial area for an
agency is *production charging*. Agencies pass on to their clients
all the outside costs incurred in the preparation of their
advertisements. Such costs include those for photography,
retouching, drawings and artwork, typesetting, film-
making and processing, actors' and models' fees and block-
making. Additionally, agencies add a commission equivalent to 15% to those costs in order to increase revenue. This
is all standard advertising agency practice.

The financial problems that arise in this area are two-
fold: firstly, work that the agency has commissioned on
behalf of a client sometimes turns out unsatisfactorily. More
difficult still, it may be thought satisfactory by the agency
but unacceptable by the client. This can be a highly subjec-
tive area; it is all too easy for several people to disagree
violently (all of them with the best of intentions) about
whether or not a photograph or drawing is excellent. If,

finally, the photograph or drawing is rejected the photographer or artist will still demand payment, though possibly at a reduced level. This kind of problem can generate considerable minor friction between clients, agencies and agencies' suppliers.

Secondly, many of an agency's production suppliers tend to be small companies with inefficient, or at the very least unsophisticated accounting systems. Photographers, artists and similar people are often not good bookkeepers. They therefore frequently send in their invoices late, or wrong, or without quoting reference numbers. And since a medium-sized agency will receive dozens of such invoices daily, sorting them out is a continuous and time-consuming chore.

So you will realise that a thoroughly capable and efficient finance department is vital to the well-being of an agency. If things start to go wrong in the finance department, the disastrous effects will soon be felt by every other department in the agency.

Having examined in some depth the functions of the six basic advertising agency departments, we must now look, a little more briefly, at each of the eight additional departments which are not to be found in every agency.

(vii) Television production

Following the inauguration of commercial television in Britain in 1955, most of the larger agencies set up specialist television production departments to supervise the making of commercials. These departments were staffed with producers who came either from the BBC or from the cinema industry. It was soon discovered, however, that most of the technical expertise necessary for the making of commercials could be found in the *film production companies*, which are not connected to agencies and exist quite independently of them.

Some agencies therefore disbanded their high-powered internal television departments, and instead employed a smaller number of television producers/co-ordinators who work within and as part of the creative department.

(viii) Merchandising and promotion

Merchandising and promotion departments exist within some large agencies to generate and organise below-the-line promotions of the kind detailed in the last chapter. Most agencies now charge fees for this work, and therefore some of the largest have hived off their merchandising and promotion departments into separate subsidiaries. Alternatively, smaller agencies expect their client contact executives to run merchandising and promotion activities for their clients.

(ix) Marketing

As we saw at the beginning of Chapter 2, marketing is a wide-ranging subject, and in reality advertising is but one aspect of marketing activity. It might therefore be considered back-to-front for an advertising agency to have a marketing department, when in fact advertising is just a department of marketing. Indeed many marketing executives in large companies take exactly this point of view.

In reality, the marketing department of an advertising agency does not aspire to make overall marketing decisions on a client's behalf; it simply aims to collate the existing information relevant to any particular market, and to analyse marketing problems and opportunities. In some agencies this role is now called *account planning*. Again this is a function which smaller agencies expect their client contact executives to carry out. One most important facet of the marketing department's activities is the collection and filing of data. Almost every agency has a data library, from the simplest to the most highly sophisticated. In some agencies, again usually the smaller ones, the data library comes under the aegis of the media department.

(x) Market research

As was stated earlier, agency market research departments —like merchandising and promotion departments, and public relations departments—are nowadays frequently run as wholly independent subsidiaries. This of course does not absolve the agency from all responsibility as to their functional efficiency. However, it obviously changes significantly the agency's relationship with them. Nevertheless large agencies still employ market research executives, to plan and co-ordinate opinion surveys, attitude analyses, product tests and advertisement tests. These executives are either separated into a specialist department or they are amalgamated with the client service department.

(xi) Personnel

Only the very largest agencies—those employing 250 people or more—have separate personnel departments. The functions of an agency personnel department are precisely the same as those of such departments elsewhere: recruitment, staff welfare, staff training and the resolving of general personal problems.

(xii) International

Obviously only an agency operating on an international basis will require a separate international department. In most agencies, which transact international business only from time to time, the work is handled once again by the relevant client service executive.

In the agencies where they exist, international departments are generally small, staffed by a director or senior executive who may be backed up by an assistant and/or a secretary. The department's function will be to co-ordinate the agency's work on its international accounts and to deal with their opposite numbers—the international marketing presidents and executives—in client companies.

(xiii) Public relations

Agency public relations departments, as has been said, are usually run as wholly independent subsidiary companies. This is for three reasons. First, the particular knowledge and expertise needed in public relations work—close contact with journalists and politicians, for example—are not normally found in an agency. Second, people who have this expertise are highly paid and agencies cannot afford to offer their services 'free' within their 15% commission. Since agencies are forced to charge for public relations work they aim to make a profit from it, and this can generally be done more effectively via a separate and independently audited company. Third, the media, whom public relations are generally trying to influence, prefer advertising to be kept quite separate from editorial and therefore rather prefer to deal with public relations companies which are independent of advertising agencies.

However, some agencies, in this case often the smaller to medium-sized ones, do offer public relations work as part of their service, either as a loss-making bonus attraction to their clients or on a non-profit-making break-even basis.

(xiv) Conferences and exhibitions

Almost all the points made above concerning merchandising, market research and public relations departments apply equally to agency conference and exhibition departments. While the practice of having such departments was quite prevalent in large agencies in the 1950s and 1960s it is now recognised that the mounting of conferences and the design of exhibitions are specialist work, best handled by specialist companies (of which there are many) with the relevant knowledge and experience. Thus few agencies now offer these services in-house, though they will always help clients with their conferences and exhibitions by recommending the best specialist companies for the job.

Organisation: How the departments function together

It is important to note two points. First, agency people are for ever meeting and discussing their clients' advertising problems in an *ad hoc* way, so that many more casual communications lines exist than can be shown on a formal chart. Second, good agency management encourages contributions from all departments on all subjects, and strongly deprecates demarcation disputes between them. The famous 'Drinka Pinta Milka Day' slogan was dreamed up by a secretary who was not even employed in the creative department!

Building a successful agency

To be successful an advertising agency must achieve three aims:

1. It must hold on to its existing clients.
2. It must make the advertising budgets of its existing clients grow.
3. It must continuously gain new clients.

To achieve these aims the agency must obviously work extremely hard, and conscientiously, and professionally, and must produce effective advertising. This is all necessary, but it is not sufficient. The very existence of advertising itself disproves Ralph Waldo Emerson's famous dictum:

> 'If a man write a better book, preach a better sermon, or make a better mouse-trap than his neighbour, though he build his house in the woods, the world will make a beaten path to his door.'

Sadly perhaps, life is not so simple. Just as advertisers must communicate the virtues of their products to customers, likewise agencies must communicate the virtues of their services to advertisers.

(i) Holding on to existing clients
There have been several studies into the subject of what clients look for from their agencies and one of the best was carried out by Lintas in 1970. (Lintas is the agency owned by Unilever which handles most of Unilever's advertising worldwide.) In the study 165 advertisers were asked to rank in order of importance 21 different aspects of agency service, and to rate each of the aspects on a four-point scale running:

1. *Essential*, 2. *Very important*, 3. *Fairly important*, 4. *Not important*.

Here are the results:

Average score

1. 'Be creatively lively.'   2·7
2. 'Able to produce original, creative ideas.'   2·7
3. 'Be really interested in the client's problems.'   2·7
4. 'Have a top class management team.'   2·5
5. 'Have a high level of understanding of your marketing problems.' 2·5
6. 'Have a very high calibre of personnel.'   2·5
7. 'Be flexible in meeting client's changing requirements.'   2·4
8. 'Have a practical consumer-orientated creative approach.'   2·3
9. 'Be progressive in outlook.'   2·3
10. 'Use research intelligently.'   2·2
11. 'Have an outstanding media department.'   2·0
12. 'Have a wide range of experienced personnel.'   2·0
13. 'Give personal attention to client at senior level.'   1·9
14. 'Allow client to deal with the people who do the actual work.' 1·8
16. 'Have a systematic approach to new product development.'   1·3
17. 'Agency should be growing and expanding.'   1·3
18. 'Be experienced in your type of market.'   1·2
19. 'Have facilities for producing below-the-line material.'   1·0
20. 'Be uninterested in winning advertising awards.'   0·7
21. 'Have a world-wide organisation.'   0·6

From which you will see that for most advertisers the all-important aspect of an agency's service is its creative ability to produce lively and original ideas for advertisements. This in turn will both depend upon and demonstrate the agency's enthusiasm and understanding for its clients' products. Personal contact and friendship, keen media buying and general efficiency, while important, are in the long run subservient to this prime requirement.

(ii) *Making existing clients' budgets grow*

This is perhaps the most essential factor in building a successful agency. It is essential because it directly earns the agency more and more commissions, sometimes without a greatly increased work input; it is essential because it establishes the clients' faith in the agency and its work; and it is essential because it proves to prospective clients that the agency produces highly effective advertising.

Making existing clients' budgets grow is a corollary of successfully *holding on to existing clients*. The same agency abilities are called for in both cases. And it points to the simplest axiom of agency growth: an agency can only be as successful as its clients; if they prosper, it will prosper; if they fail, it will fail.

(iii) *Winning new clients*

More nonsense is propagated about the process of winning new clients than about any other aspect of the advertising agency business. Hollywood movies have depicted it as a combination of high-powered salesmanship, seduction, sex and silliness. Agencies are believed to keep secret dossiers of prospective clients' whims and desires, particularly the naughtier ones, and to be ready to pander to them at the drop of a rumour. The truth is more mundane.

Winning new clients is hard, time-consuming work. Certainly efficient agencies do keep files on prospective clients. But the files will be stacked full of every scrap of marketing data relevant to the client's business which the agency can find; sometimes (rarely) are added a few personal details about the client of the most innocuous kind. (Married or single? Children? Where he lives, hobbies etc.) Certainly agencies 'entertain' prospective clients inviting them to their premises for drinks, or out for lunch or dinner or to a show. But the vast majority of clients are exceptionally cautious about being wined and dined too much by agencies. Reputations spread quickly both within the agency world and, much more importantly, within clients' own companies. Nobody respects a freeloader. Certainly many agencies designate one director or senior executive as being in charge of winning new clients, and he will need to be a super-salesman: fast-talking, friendly, knowledgeable, charming and not a little thick-skinned. But it is not the glamorous, fulfilling job that many agency people aspire to; on the contrary, it is often a niche invented for an account director who would otherwise have too little to do.

Having dispensed with the myths, let us concentrate upon the realities. Over the last 20 years the most successful agencies in both London and New York have been those that have consistently produced effective advertising and have communicated this fact to prospective clients. They communicate with prospective clients by direct mail, telephone, PR in the trade press and sometimes, though comparatively rarely, by advertising themselves. What do they aim to communicate? Each agency will, of course, promote its own advantages. But a small survey carried out by an agency called Scientific Advertising and Marketing Ltd. showed, firstly, why agencies are *short-listed* by clients thinking of moving their account. The answers were as follows:

Reasons for Short-listing
1. Creativity
2. Experience
3. No competitive client conflict
4. Reputation
5. Size

6. International (where relevant)
7. Management

Very rarely will a prospective client appoint a new agency without visiting several on his short-list, and soliciting presentations for his account from the best of those short-listed. The presentation may merely consist of a demonstration of the agency itself: its organisation, its personnel, its record and its work. Or more usually it will also include a preliminary analysis by the agency of the client's marketing problems and opportunities. This will involve the agency in much work and effort. The client may have produced a detailed written brief for the agency, but it is more likely that the agency will need to brief itself.

In addition to the aforementioned data files, which will now prove their worth, the agency will rapidly aim to indoctrinate itself and immerse itself in all aspects of the client's operation. Normally only 4–8 weeks will be available for the preparation of the presentation. Obviously the amount of work the agency puts in will be roughly proportional to the size of the prospective client's account (or, more accurately, to the size of the account in comparison with the size of the agency itself).

For an account which it really wishes to win the agency may carry out any or all of the following ten activities:

(a) Pilot consumer research
(b) Full-scale consumer research
(c) Sales analyses, both historical and regional
(d) Marketing operations study
(e) Trade research
(f) Factory tours
(g) Store visits with client's representatives
(h) Product and competitive product consumer tests and analyses
(i) Advertising analyses
(j) Advertising research

Having studied and analysed all of this information the agency may then prepare specific proposals and recommendations for the prospective client. These are likely to cover:

(a) Marketing strategy and objectives;
(b) Media strategy and recommendations;
(c) Below-the-line promotional ideas and recommendations;
(d) Creative strategy and, finally . . .
(e) Speculative creative proposals.

There is much debate within the advertising agency business as to whether or not it is right for agencies to prepare speculative creative proposals for prospective clients. The protagonists for doing so argue that there is no better way to help a client judge which new agency is going to be the best one for his company. The antagonists claim that such work is always done too quickly, based on insufficient knowledge, is rarely if ever finally used, and takes agency creative people away from working for the agency's existing clients who thereby suffer in the process.

Whatever the pros and cons of the argument, the practical reality is that virtually every agency will prepare creative work for a prospective client it wants badly enough. And some agencies quite enjoy doing creative work for prospective clients, since they are less shackled by historical and political considerations than is often the case with existing clients.

Incidentally, prospective clients are expected to pay agencies a fee if speculative creative work is produced, and most do so; but the fee, though welcome to the agency, almost never covers the actual costs involved.

When the agency has completed its study of the data and produced its recommendations and proposals, it is ready to make a *presentation* to the client. New client presentations are one of the most exciting features of advertising agency life. If an important new client is coming on a visit, everyone in the agency will know. Memos will be circulated, offices will be cleaned and tidied, those involved in the presentation will be especially excited—and probably slightly nervous. The presentation may last anything from an hour to a whole day, and may include the use of slides, charts, films, video-tape, overhead projection, and all of the most modern paraphernalia of audio-visual communication.

Once it is over, how does the prospective client make up his mind and sort out the hard content from the razzama-tazz? The Scientific Advertising and Marketing Survey previously referred to also examined this point. The clients interviewed gave these answers:

> *Reasons for agency appointment*
> 1. Understand client's problems
> 2. Creative
> 3. Management
> 4. Ability
> 5. Compatibility
> 6. Presentation and record
> 7. Size of agency

These answers demonstrate that the mythical frenetic chase for new clients can be reduced to straightforward, intelligent and relevant dimensions: understanding, creativity, management, ability and compatibility. If an agency can demonstrate all those characteristics it will certainly be successful, and rightly so.

Think Exercises

1. You decide to set up your own agency and knowing how competitive the business is, you decide to offer extra services that other agencies don't. Think of two services not mentioned in this chapter which you could offer to clients, peripheral to advertising but nevertheless relevant.
2. 'Advertising agencies are an anachronism,' said the management consultant. 'Their work could be better done either by the clients—who know all about their

products and their markets; or by the media—who are experts in communication.' Try to refute the apparent logic of his case with convincing arguments.

3. Be your own job analyst! If you are interested in advertising then you are almost certainly interested in people and in ideas. But all of the jobs in an agency require other aptitudes and abilities as well. List the main jobs and write down next to each of them what you think *your* strengths and *your* weaknesses would be if you found yourself doing one of them.

5
Planning a Campaign

You have now been introduced to all the elements of the advertising industry and so the time has come to see how they work together to produce effective advertisements. That is the subject matter of this chapter, which is divided into the following nine sections:

    (*i*) *Setting the objectives*
    (*ii*) *How much should be spent?*
  (*iii*) *Where should it be spent?*
  (*iv*) *What should the advertisements say?*
    (*v*) *How should they say it?*
  (*vi*) *Creating the advertisements*
  (*vii*) *Executing the advertisements*
(*viii*) *Producing the advertisements*
  (*ix*) *Who does what?*

Before starting it is necessary to repeat a proviso with which you may by now be becoming all too familiar: there are many different types of advertising and many different types of advertiser. Inevitably the process of producing advertising varies from one to another. It is not sensible (or even possible) to go through exactly the same procedures prior to producing a classified for a secondhand car and prior to producing a 30-second detergent commercial. This chapter will primarily consider the development of national advertising for major advertisers. You yourself will need to keep in mind that, as you have seen, this is by no means the entirety of the advertising business.

Setting the objectives

This patently obvious all-important first step in the proceedings is, regrettably, one which is frequently skipped over
too lightly. This is because of the nebulous nature of advertising and of the difficulties involved in accurately measuring
its results. Some people feel that there is little point in setting
objectives if you cannot at the end measure whether or not
you have achieved them.

There are two answers to this argument. First, as we shall
see in Chapter 6, it is frequently possible to measure many
of the effects of advertising if sufficient care is taken and
planning is carried out in advance. Second, the very discipline of analysing and setting down objectives sharpens
thinking and increases the likelihood that the advertising
will be effective, even if the degree of its effectiveness cannot
be precisely measured.

Before objectives can be determined it is essential for the
agency, in partnership with the client, to study and consider carefully all the data mentioned in the paragraphs on
How to Win New Accounts, and much more. Once the
agency has been awarded the account it will be privy to the
client's turnover and profit figures, analysed historically,
seasonally and regionally. The agency will also be shown the
market surveys that the client has carried out, and these
surveys will often stretch back over some years. The agency
will also be in a position to get to know intimately what the
client has learned, perhaps over decades, about consumers'
usage of his own and competitive products, and about which
advertising approaches have worked and which have not.
All of this the agency must digest and understand in order
that realistic objectives can be set.

Objectives can then be defined in terms of several criteria.

(i) *Increasing awareness*—There are only a few products of
which all potential customers are already aware. Guinness,
Heinz Baked Beans, Coke and Pepsi, Embassy & Players

No. 6 cigarettes, Tide, Surf and Omo and a short list of other famous names will be among them. But for most advertisers one main purpose of their advertising is to increase people's knowledge of their existence. This objective can be defined and measured with accuracy. Through market research it is easily possible to establish how many people have heard of a brand or company; by repeating the research after the advertising has appeared the increase in *awareness* achieved can be quantified.

Awareness can be measured in two ways, *spontaneous* and *prompted*. The *spontaneous awareness* will show the number of people mentioning each particular name in answer to the open-ended question: '*Tell me all the makes of detergent you have heard of. Any more? Is that all?*'

For *prompted awareness* the respondent will be shown a printed list of all the detergents on the market and asked which she has ever heard of. The human memory being what it is, *prompted* awareness figures are invariably higher than *spontaneous* awareness figures.

Awareness objectives can be set and measured thus:

	Pre-campaign		Objectives		Post-campaign achieved	
	Spont.	Prompt.	Spont.	Prompt.	Spont.	Prompt.
Brand X	17%	29%	30%	45%	28%	39%

In this example the campaign came close to achieving the objectives set but did not quite do so. Further advertising would be required if the targeted objectives are to be reached.

(*ii*) *Changing attitudes*—This is a far more complex area to research. However, the basic principle is straightforward. Increasing awareness may be of little importance on its own; when people hear about your brand they may not like what they have heard. The classic example of this situation was *Strand* cigarettes. Launched in the early 1960s with an outstandingly memorable advertising campaign, within weeks over 90 % of smokers were *aware* of *Strand*. But the more they heard about it, the less they liked it. The advertising showed a silent man in a raincoat wandering on his own late at night through London's rain-soaked streets, smoking a *Strand* for solace. The slogan ran 'You're never alone with a Strand'.

The advertising was technically brilliant, and created great impact. Unhappily it reminded smokers of the worst aspects of their habit. Smokers feel guilty about smoking alone; and the lonely figure appeared to have no home, no friends, and no success. As a result the campaign was a disaster. *Strand* did not sell and was soon withdrawn from the market.

Strand was a famous extreme case. With the possible exception of the notorious Ford *Edsel* car—which was launched in 1957 in the United States with massive publicity, but failed to sell more than a few thousand cars—no other brand or maker has achieved such well-publicised failure so quickly. Nevertheless both examples emphasise a truth that on a lesser scale advertisers frequently discover: if a product or its advertising is wrong, the greater the awareness achieved the more speedy will be its demise. For this reason the measurement of *awareness* alone can often be misleading. The aim of most advertising is not merely to inform (make aware) but to persuade (change attitudes).

Therefore sophisticated advertisers with sufficient market research resources measure not merely changes in awareness but also changes in attitudes. Before their campaign they discover what the public's views of their own and competitive makes are. To quantify these views mathematically, *rating scales* are used. Rating scales are calibrated lines with opposite descriptions at each end, such as:

Excellent Quality   **Very bad Quality**

```
|-------|-------|-------|-------|-------|-------|
1       2       3       4       5       6       7
```

Respondents are asked to place different brands or makes in position on the scale. The views of say, 500 respondents will be obtained for each make and from these average or *mean scores* can be calculated. These scores will then show which makes the public thinks are better quality, which worse, and, most importantly, these attitudes will have a numerical value. Scores will be obtained on several relevant attitudinal dimensions. For a beer, for example, in addition to *excellent quality/very bad quality* the scales might also cover:

Very strong	......	Very weak
Exceptionally nice taste	......	Exceptionally nasty taste
Expensive	......	Cheap
Only drunk by men	......	Only drunk by women
Very gassy	......	Very flat

The advertising objectives would then be set in terms of changing consumers' attitudes, to a targeted degree, on the rating scales. Whether or not the objectives were achieved could thus be measured.

(*iii*) *Generating direct response*—In the realm of direct response advertising, objectives can be set most exactly. Past results will usually be an excellent guide to future response. Additionally, it is almost always possible in direct response advertising to calculate just what percentage of sales revenue can be spent on advertising; and a fundamental objective is not to exceed this advertising-to-sales percentage ratio—for if it is exceeded the advertising must be running at a loss.

However, there will often be subsidiary, less overt, objectives which the direct response advertisements are intended to achieve. The advertising will usually be intended to increase the public's level of awareness of the advertiser, since future response rates will be improved if the public knows who the advertiser is. The advertising will also be intended to enhance the advertiser's general image—just as manufacturer's brand advertising does—since future response rates will also improve if the public trusts the advertiser and can feel confident about the goods being advertised.

To measure the effects of his advertising in terms of awareness and image (or attitudes) the direct response advertiser would also need to carry out market surveys. Whether or not he carries out such surveys, the wise direct response advertiser will always keep in his mind these subsidiary objectives when planning his advertising.

(iv) *Sales increases*—For most advertisers this is the only objective that really counts. All other objectives are necessarily substitutes for this, the intrinsic aim and purpose of the bulk of advertising. Unfortunately, there are too many variables in the marketing process for advertisers generally to be able to draw a direct correlation between sales and advertising. The activities of competitors, the efficiency of their own sales force, retailers' actions, the economy at large, fashions, population trends (and even the weather) may separately and together influence sales both in the short and long-term. The direct inter-relationship between advertising and sales can rarely be isolated. That is why advertisers have turned to such indirect yardsticks as 'awareness' and 'attitude change' where the particular effects of advertising alone can be measured.

Nevertheless, as has been stated, although there may be no method of knowing whether or not an objective has been achieved it is still frequently worth while to set targets. In fact almost all advertisers do aim to reach specific sales objectives each year and recognise that their advertising will be one of the several inputs that will help them to achieve these objectives. (Although this section has been titled *Sales increases* the objective of much advertising is the lesser one of minimising or reversing *sales decline*.)

These objectives may be defined in absolute terms, or with reference to the advertiser's *market share*. In absolute terms the objectives would be stated as follows: 'To help increase sales in 1978 over those in 1977 by X%.' Or 'To help halt this year's sales decline of Y% and thus achieve level sales next year.'

In *market share* terms the objectives would be stated as follows: 'To help increase Brand A's share of the tinned catfood market from 7·3% in 1977 to 8·5% in 1978.' Or, 'To help reverse brand B's loss of 1·6% share of the analgesic market this year, by gaining 0·5% in market share next year.'

These objectives are not strictly advertising objectives, though they will often be found in advertising plans.

However, there is one situation in which sales targets can be and are used as the defined advertising objectives. This is in test markets or regional advertising. Here all the other variables are kept constant in other areas of the country so that—unless for some freak reason the test region behaves peculiarly—the sales achieved in the region can be positively correlated with the advertising.

(*v*) *Other objectives*—In addition to the prime objectives listed above, advertising is often used to achieve other aims. Usually these are subsidiary to its main purposes but they may nevertheless carry considerable weight. Such objectives include:

    (*a*) encouraging retailers to stock the advertised brand;

    (*b*) improving and encouraging staff morale (particularly for the sales force);

    (*c*) reassuring existing customers that they have made the right decision; and possibly encouraging them to use more;

    (*d*) keeping the cost of entry into the market high to deter new competition.

These are the objectives. Now we must turn to the question of advertising costs.

How much should be spent?

There are many methods of setting an advertising budget. Here we shall consider the seven most commonly used. All stem from the basic objectives that have been defined above; if you keep these in mind you will more easily grasp the advantages and disadvantages of each method.

Method 1: Fixed percentage of past year's sales.

Advantages: Little short-term financial risk; the money to be spent has already been earned.

Disadvantages: Will result in financial loss if sales are rapidly declining; and will perpetuate declining sales but retard speed of growth if sales are increasing. Takes no account of competitive or other market activity.

Method 2: Fixed percentage of next year's projected sales.

Advantages: Takes account of likely changes in market and sales trends. Encourages understanding of the advertising/sales correlation.

Disadvantages: As for method 1, will tend to perpetuate declining sales while retarding growth of increasing sales. Also takes no account of competitive or other market activity.

Method 3: Whatever the company can afford.

Advantages: Allows company to transfer promotional funds

flexibly from one product to another as business and marketing situations dictate. Minimises risk of loss.

Disadvantages: By definition rules out investing for growth. Once again takes no account of competitive or other market activity.

Method 4: Appropriation based on competitors' spending.
Advantages: Takes account of activity in the market place. Relates appropriation to consumers' likely frequency of perception of competitive campaigns.
Disadvantages: Can promote costly advertising expenditure wars between competitors. Takes no direct account of advertiser's own financial situation.

Method 5: Promotional/profit joint residuum.
Advantages: Allows advertiser flexibility to increase or decrease proportion of sales revenue after costs to be spent on advertising and promotion. Directly involves profits and profitability in the calculations.
Disadvantages: Again takes no account of competitive or market activity. Too 'self-orientated'; tempts advertiser to make extra short-term profit by cutting advertising budget.

Method 6: Budget based on target market share.
Advantages: Research has proved there to be a long-term correlation in most markets between share of advertising and share of market. Takes account of competitive activity.
Disadvantages: Takes no direct account of advertiser's own financial situation. Likely to involve investment/reduced short-term profits.

Method 7: Budget based on coverage/frequency communications' objectives.
Advantages: Generally considered most sophisticated approach. Relates campaign to consumer perceptions. Can be compared with competitors' coverage/frequency patterns.
Disadvantages: Takes no direct account of advertiser's own financial situation. Precise coverage/frequency objectives often difficult to establish.

In practice the great majority of advertisers use a combination of methods, and appraise their budget from several standpoints. In smaller companies methods 1 and 2 are most commonly practised. Larger companies, spending more money, usually incorporate methods 5, 6 and 7. They calculate how much it will cost to achieve a particular market share on the basis of target communications objectives; they then consider the financial implications of such an expenditure in profit terms. If this outcome is unsatisfactory, they review the target market share and communications objectives. Looking at the problem from these various angles, and analysing the likely results in market share, profit and communications terms of varying levels of expenditure, the best overall level is eventually determined.

Where should it be spent?

In Chapter 3 we discussed the broad advantages and disadvantages of each of the media. Now we must consider how the advertiser decides exactly which media will be best for his purposes. This process is called *media selection*. The four most important criteria involved in *media selection* are:

    (*i*) Budget;
   (*ii*) Target market;
  (*iii*) Regionality and seasonability;
  (*iv*) Media characteristics—flexibility, colour, movement, sound, atmosphere.

(*i*) *Budget*. The size of the advertising budget may in itself rule out the possibility of using certain media. That is one of the reasons why experienced advertisers pay so much attention to calculating it carefully and consider the matter from so many different angles.

For a national campaign for a *non-seasonal* product or service, the minimum levels of annual advertising expenditure are widely accepted to be:

Television: £300,000 a year
Posters : £150,000 a year
Cinema : £100,000 a year
Radio : £30,000 a year

There is no equivalent figure for the press, magazines, below-the-line, direct mail or the mini-media because these are so highly flexible, and offer the advertiser an infinite range of levels of circulation, space size, and possible frequency. Nevertheless even in these media certain rules-of-thumb apply. Most advertisers would agree that it is unwise to deploy an annual budget of less than £20,000 in the mass-circulation newspapers and magazines, even if very small spaces are used.

(*ii*) *Target market*. The accurate establishment of the correct *target market* for an advertising campaign is unquestionably one of the most important steps in campaign planning. Proctor and Gamble, the mammoth American toiletries and detergent company, makes this point clearly by stating that one advertisement may be better or worse than another, but no matter how good the advertisement may be, if it is shown to the wrong people it simply cannot work. The most brilliantly effective dogfood commercial ever created will be totally wasted on an audience with no dogs!

The *target market* for any product or service is defined as that section of the population most likely to buy the product (or use the service) in a foreseeable period of time. It may be that the target market comprises people who already use the product, and are being encouraged to use it more often. It may be that the target market will take many months to make up its mind on a purchase decision—as is usually the case with expensive consumer durables. It may be that the target market is by its nature ever-changing—as is the case with products for tiny babies. The target market may be extremely broad and encompass a large proportion of the population—as would usually be the case with cigarettes or toothpaste or beer; or the target market may be extremely

narrow and difficult to identify and reach really economically—as is the case with many partwork publications, some
liqueurs and most consumer durables.

How can the target market be defined? In the simplest
cases, the answer is straightforward logic. The target market
for baby products must obviously be pregnant women and
new mothers; the target market for Rolls-Royce cars will
obviously be the extremely wealthy. Sadly the great majority of cases are not so simple. In these cases the advertiser
can add hunch and intuition to his logic—the target market
for powerful binoculars will certainly include ornithologists,
among others; the target market for a denture cleanser will
include older rather than younger people. If, however, the
advertiser requires more precision in the definition of his
target market, he will need to call for market research.
Nowadays it is extremely likely that an advertiser promoting
any but the most esoteric of products will be able to purchase existing market research that will tell him almost all
he needs to know. Much information can be obtained from
the JICNARS National Readership Surveys. Otherwise the
most likely sources of research data are the following:

British Market Research Bureau—Each year, and on a continuing basis, the British Market Research Bureau Limited
(BMRB) surveys 30,000 homes in the U.K. and publishes a
study called the *Target Group Index* (TGI). TGI is now almost certainly the most widely used research survey in
Britain; and it is also widely used in the U.S.A., where
BMRB's sister company in New York, Axiom Market
Research Bureau (AMRB) runs an identical American
edition of TGI. In both the U.K. and U.S.A., TGI covers
an extraordinary breadth of products and services including:

Beers	Spirits
Cigarettes	Unit Trusts
Toilet soaps	Building Societies
Detergents	Cars
Wines	Petrols

Shampoos

Petfoods

Soups

Toothpastes

Margarines

Squashes

Slimming products

Bath additives

Carbonated drinks

Washing machines

Refrigerators

Vacuum cleaners

Home ownership

Men's toiletries

For each product field it gives the following types of information, analysed in the most relevant way for every product:

Number of users

Heavy/Medium/Light Users

Demographic profile of users—by age, sex, region, class

Certain basic attitudes of users

'Solus' users (who use that brand or product only)

Recency of purchase (for consumer durables)

Readership of users

TV viewing of users

All of this data is cross-analysed into subgroups in an almost infinite variety of ways. Any advertiser or agency can purchase TGI analyses according to a scale rate of fees. But TGI is so frequently used and published that an assiduous search will often produce snippets of usable data which (no doubt to the research company's chagrin) the advertiser may be able to obtain without cost.

National Opinion Polls—Unlike BMRB, National Opinion Polls Limited (NOP) do not run a single, continuous major survey but instead carry out throughout the year numerous specialised *ad hoc* surveys—looking into particular aspects of marketing such as Christmas gifts (who gives what, to whom, and how much do they spend on it). A list of its current surveys can always be obtained from NOP and, again, they can be purchased inexpensively usually for only a few hundred pounds each.

Economist Intelligence Unit—The EIU produces a number of authoritative publications which cover a wide range of subjects and markets. The most useful publication, for the general advertiser, is a monthly called *Retail Business*. Every month *Retail Business* will contain long and comprehensive reports on four or five consumer goods' markets, and these reports will contain a wealth of information culled from various sources including government statistics and, quite often, the EIU's own market surveys. When first approaching a market or product field about which you have no previous knowledge it is always a good idea to go to the EIU and *Retail Business* first. Over nearly twenty years they have published in excess of 1,400 individual reports, and there is no sounder way of quickly obtaining a general understanding of what is happening in many markets.

In addition to *Retail Business* the EIU publishes seven other important regular journals including *Motor Business* (quarterly), *Multinational Business* (quarterly), *Marketing in Europe* (monthly), and *European Trends* (quarterly with an annual supplement).

Mintel—Like the EIU, Mintel publishes a regular monthly journal which reports on recent activities and trends in a wide spectrum of markets. Mintel's reports, unlike the EIU's, tend to be less concerned with summarising and digesting government economic statistics (though Mintel certainly pays close attention to those that are relevant).

Instead they are more concerned with consumers' habits and attitudes which they always establish through their own market surveys. Inevitably, because both the EIU and Mintel look at only forty to fifty markets per year, in some instances the EIU will have published the more recent study, in other cases Mintel will have done so.

TGI, NOP, the EIU and Mintel by no means exhaust the list of sources of published and purchaseable market data which can help the advertiser to define his target market. There are innumerable others, mostly much smaller. An efficient advertising agency library will keep track of these, and have them carefully filed and indexed. But what happens if, after obtaining and studying all the available information, the advertiser is still unable to define his target market sufficiently precisely? Perhaps he is bringing out a revolutionary new product, which by definition cannot have been researched before; or perhaps he is looking for a deep insight to help him define his prospective customers characteristics in ways which none of the broad-spectrum surveys have covered.

In this situation he must commission his own market research, tailored specifically to meet his own particular needs. This is not the place to examine the intricacies of market research, about which many good books have been published (see the bibliography). Suffice it to say here that if you have little or no experience of commissioning market research the wisest course is to approach the Market Research Society, 15, Belgrave Square, London S.W.1.—the professional body to which every reputable market research company in the country belongs. Explain the problem briefly to them and they will nominate four or five companies perfectly qualified to handle it. Approach these nominated companies, brief them, and you will obtain from each a detailed research proposal on the basis of which you will be able to make a sound choice.

Sufficient data having been analysed, how will the target market be defined? First, and most importantly, *demographically*: in terms of age, sex, region, socio-economic class, marital status and possibly number of children; second, in terms of ownership of relevant other goods—automobile ownership for petrol, tyres, spares, car insurance etc; third, in terms of relevant characteristic habits: heavy/light users of detergents, frequent/infrequent visitors to dry cleaners, for example; fourth, in terms of current usage of competitive products: i.e. specifying the products people are using which you aim to persuade them to exchange for your own; fifth, in terms of any known psychological and attitudinal variables which will help complete the identikit picture of your likely prospective consumer.

The target market for the launch of an imaginary new strong-but-gentle washing powder might be defined as below:

Age	:	25–44
Sex	:	Female
Region	:	London and South East
Class	:	ABC1 C2
Marital Status	:	Married
Children	:	Yes
Ownership	:	Washing machine
Usership	:	Heavy user of washing powders
Current Brand is:		Fairy Snow, Dreft.
Characteristics	:	Extremely concerned about whiteness, cleanliness and hygiene but *also* concerned about effects of detergents on materials and on skin.

(Still more advanced target market analyses will give numerical weightings to each of these various factors, so that their relative importance can be assessed mathematically.)

With the picture now reasonably complete, the media planner is in a position to identify the media that will reach the target market most cost-effectively. To do this he will prepare various alternative media proposals, all of course within the predetermined budget, and compare them. He may well require the aid of a computer, because of the multiplicity of options and the complexity of the arithmetic. For each schedule he will need to know:

1. The percentage of the target market who will be reached by the campaign (*coverage*);
2. The number of times they will have an opportunity to see the advertising (*frequency*);
3. The cost per thousand impacts (*the cheaper the cost the better*).

These are the basic facts and figures on which media plans are based.

(*iii*) *Regionality and seasonality*. Regionality and seasonality are in some respects sub-divisions of the target market definition. Both the time of year when customers buy a product and the areas where they live must obviously be included in the target market identikit portrait. However, these two aspects of the target market have an additional significance in media planning because they inter-relate directly with the budget and can sometimes have a decisive influence on the choice of medium.

Let us look at how this happens, taking regionality first. As we have seen, the minimum effective annual budget for a national television campaign is approximately £300,000. If, however, the advertiser only needs to cover one small region of the country this sum will be greatly reduced. The equivalent minimum in Tyne-Tees would be approximately £21,000, in Anglia less than £11,000. Thus quite small budgets can buy heavy campaigns in expensive media if used regionally.

Of equal importance is the fact that in many cases a local marketing situation necessitates the use of local media. It makes no sense for a retailer operating in only one part of the country to advertise in another. A retailer with, for example, four or five shops in Banbury has comparatively little choice in the media he can use, however precisely he defines his target market. Television is not suitable and neither are radio, national press and magazines. The high capital cost of making a cinema commercial is likely to rule out that medium too. This still leaves posters, local press and many mini-media to choose from; but the *regionality* of the retailer's business has effectively made many of the media selection decisions for him.

Similarly, fairly small budgets can be effective in expensive media for highly seasonal products. Suntan lotions, fireworks, Christmas gifts and January Sales all call for short, intense campaigns which rarely need to last more than six weeks. In so compressed a period, a national television campaign of £80,000–£100,000 can often work successfully; and brief, inexpensive bursts of advertising in the national press can also generate immediate results. Of course, even for less seasonal products the annual pattern of sales will need to be reflected in the pattern of advertising expenditure. Sausages and soups are consumed all the year round, but more heavily in winter than in summer, whereas for soft drinks and salad-creams exactly the converse is the case. Advertising expenditure patterns reflect these trends—and possibly even exaggerate them—but the campaigns involved are usually too protracted for minimum appropriation levels to be used.

(*iv*) *Media characteristics.* The fourth area to consider in deciding in which media the advertising should be placed is the technological nature of the medium itself. As we saw at the end of Chapter 3 where the advantages and disadvantages of the different media were analysed, some offer colour, some sound, some movement, some none of these. Research has shown that the actual nature of the medium affects the way the viewer receives and reacts to the advertising message. Even if it were possible to produce precisely the same message in both a 30-second TV commercial and in the Personal Column of *The Times*, the public would react to the two communications quite differently. We bring to advertising, as to all other forms of communication, our own personal preconceptions and predispositions. We automatically (usually subconsciously) associate the advertisements we see with the media in which we see them. This halo effect is the basis of Professor Marshall McLuhan's famous dictum, 'The medium is the message'*—an exaggeration, of course, but one with a firm basis in reality.

We have already analysed the varying characteristics of

* See Professor McLuhan's now classic book 'Understanding Media' (Sphere Books, 1968).

different media. Here we must examine how these characteristics influence advertisers in choosing which media are, and are not, particularly appropriate to carry their message. The five most important media characteristics are:

(*a*) time flexibility
(*b*) colour availability
(*c*) sound
(*d*) movement
(*e*) atmosphere

Little research has been done, or in reality is needed, to help advertisers decide which of these are important to them and which are not. Intelligence and careful thought are generally sufficient. Here is a list of advertisers to whom the above characteristics are likely to matter significantly:

Time flexibility	*Colour*	*Sound*	*Movement*	*Atmosphere*
Financial	Fashion	Records	D-I-Y	Prestige
Recruitment	Cosmetics		Demonstration	'Personal'
Retail	Food		products	products
			Cookery	Fashion
			Toys	

It must be remembered that cost and target market considerations generally override media characteristics in the decision-making process. In practice, television and cinema are the only major media offering *movement*; and if these are too expensive the advertiser may have to forego the use of this characteristic no matter how desirable it may be. But when other things are equal, the characteristics of the medium *as a medium* may well tip the balance in a choice between possible alternatives.

Before leaving the subject of *media selection* it is important to note one last complexity. We have treated media selection as an isolated process, carried out in a somewhat desiccated, computerised way. In practice emotions frequently (and often rightly) enter into media selection decisions. Advertisers and their agencies get a 'feel' for their media over the years, and may disregard—or at least minimise—perfectly accurate statistics where experience has taught them that the statistics lead inexorably to the wrong conclusions. Media selection, though more mathematically precise than other aspects of advertising, is still a long way from being a predictive science.

What should the advertisements say?

This is the next stage in the planning of a campaign. The clearest explanation of what is involved is based upon the separation of form from content. In theory—though it is often intensely difficult in practice—it is possible to separate the plot and message (content) of, say *Macbeth* from the particular words and way in which they are said (form). So it is with advertising. Before advertisements are created, advertisers and their agencies seek to define most precisely the messages that they intend the target market to glean from them. This is called defining the *creative strategy*.

The key factors in the development of creative strategy are:

(*i*) The physical attributes of the product or service, and the related consumer benefits they produce;

(*ii*) Market research data showing consumers' satisfactions and dissatisfactions with their own and competitors' products/services;

(*iii*) Previous advertising history and competitors' advertising claims.

Let us briefly examine how each of these can contribute to the creative strategy.

(*i*) *Physical attributes and consumer benefits*. The most simplistic consumerists' and economists' view that goods and services are nothing more than their physical and chemical specifications takes no account of human emotions and values. Of course, the physical attributes of a product are almost always of importance to consumers. They are probably of least importance in such fields as cosmetics and fashion.

(Few care what the chemical composition of a lipstick or a tie is. It is the colours and patterns that count.) They are of greatest importance in motor cars and other consumer durables (which is why many car advertisements and all car leaflets contain lengthy technical specifications).

Between the extremes, most goods provide both physical and psychological benefits to their users, and the creative strategy must define so far as possible exactly what these are. This can be surprisingly difficult, since even the overtly physical benefits usually only make real sense in terms of complex human needs and gratifications. To exaggerate, nobody has a real need for nails, but lots of people have a need to join pieces of wood together; few people particularly want to acquire gramophone records but many enjoy listening to reproduced music; nobody wants packets of seeds, but gardeners love growing and looking at plants. This differentiation between *physical attributes* and the *end benefits* they produce is crucial in all aspects of marketing and particularly in the development of creative strategy. Clearly the physical attributes and the end benefits inter-relate; you can't have one without the other. But they are not the same things, and they must always be carefully distinguished.

(ii) Consumers' satisfactions and dissatisfactions. No product is ideally designed to suit everybody. Mass-produced products are, by definition, used by masses of people. Thus they inevitably involve compromise. They could be made better, but then they would be more expensive. They could be made, say, to taste stronger or milder or sweeter or more bitter; in which case they would probably appeal to fewer people—but quite possibly those people would like them more. In formulating his product the manufacturer will balance the questions of cost, quality, potential volume of demand and potential strength of demand. The end result will not be perfect for everybody but, if the product is successful, will be highly acceptable to many.

In order to discover accurately how many people use his

product or service, how many use his competitors', and what users and non-users think and feel about all the products available, the manufacturer will again need market research. As in the definition of the *target market* it may be possible to obtain some of this information from published sources. It is more likely, however, that the manufacturer will need to commission his own survey if he wishes to cover this ground thoroughly.

Having obtained the data the advertiser can then summarise the strengths and weaknesses of his own and competitive products in terms of consumers' attitudes to them. Here for example, is a table showing how consumers in the U.K. might *view* five leading international airlines:

British Airways	*Pan Am*	*Lufthansa*
Fairly punctual	Punctual	Very punctual
Interesting on board	More interesting	Uninteresting on board
Pleasant staff	Impersonal staff	Impersonal clinical
Poor food	Good plain food	Plain heavy food
Moderate comfort	Comfortable	Comfortable
Safe	Very safe	Very safe

Air France	*KLM*
Not punctual	Very punctual
Interesting on board	Fairly interesting
Friendly staff	Friendly staff
Excellent food	Good food
Very comfortable	Comfortable
Fairly safe	Very safe

Two important conclusions can be drawn from this chart. First, additional market research questions will be required to answer which attitudes are most important, and to what proportion of airline travellers. A question or series of questions to this effect should invariably be included in the market research survey and will produce answers in this form:

	Percentage of airline travellers naming characteristic as 'most important'
Safety	41%
Punctuality	29%
Food	13%
Comfort	9%
Staff	5%
Interest/activity on board	3%

(It may be surprising to you that not everybody automatically rates 'safety' first; this is because experienced air travellers take this for granted—and do not allow themselves to question it!)

Second, the attitudes of air travellers to the airlines are only partially dependent upon the realities of each airline's performance. Their attitudes are obviously greatly influenced by their images of the national characteristics of the airline's country. Likewise, as we have seen before, consumers' attitudes to different brands and even to different retail chains will be influenced by many factors apart from the physical and functional realities. It is the job of market research to uncover and analyse these important attitudes and feelings.

With the benefit of this data the advertiser and his agency can define the strengths and weaknesses of the products on the market; and thus he will arrive at the satisfactions (and dissatisfactions) they generate and will know how many people like each, and why. He will also know, if the research has been carried out correctly, who the various groups of people are, and thus will be able to determine the particular reactions of the target market. The conclusions to be drawn from this information will further help him in the formulation of his creative strategy.

(*iii*) *Previous and competitive advertising.* This is the simplest and most straightforward part of the development of the creative strategy. Clearly it is essential to know what the past advertising for your product or service has been. Except in quite exceptional circumstances it would be foolhardy to contradict, or even change radically, the previous advertising strategy. This course of action is bound to confuse consumers and may even cause your existing customers to cease purchasing your goods. (This rule must not, however, be confused with the need to change the advertising interpretation—form—from time to time while the strategy—content—remains constant.)

Equally clearly it is essential to know what your competitors' advertising strategy is. Despite the contrary views of cynics, no wise advertiser ever treads the same path as a competitor. Sometimes the differences will be marginal. To people who are not conversant with the market, such marginal differences may not be visible. But inevitably any advertiser who copies exactly a competitor's strategy will run a severe danger of selling that competitor's product. That is not a risk that sensible advertisers are prepared to take.

For ease of study it is common to chart competitors' advertising thus:

Product	*Advertising Message*	*Creative Strategy*
Toilet Soap X	'Soft, gentle X is kind to your face, kind to your hands'.	X is positioned for women concerned about the drying/ageing effects of washing their skin.
Toilet Soap Y	'All day you'll smell fresh, all day you'll feel healthy, with new effective deodorant Y'.	Y is positioned for those concerned to remove all body odours when they wash, and to keep such odours at bay all day.

It is worth noting here that while competitors' advertising messages can be obtained and recorded from their published advertisements, competitors' creative strategies can only be surmised. Experienced advertising people, however, with knowledge of the relevant market, can usually make a fairly reliable guess at what their competitors' strategies are.

In the light of all the above thinking and analysis, it will now be possible for the advertiser and his agency to determine exactly what the advertisements should say i.e. to define the creative strategy. Every company has its own individual formula for how creative strategies must be written, but here are three examples of the kind that you would find in modern marketing reports.

Perfume A:
A will be positioned as a heavy, sophisticated, seductive, evening perfume, to be worn on special occasions (because of its price); advertisements must encourage it as a gift, from a man to a woman with whom he has an especially close relationship.

Brandy B:
B is currently seen as not being an authentic French brandy. Advertising must communicate the authenticity, tradition and origins of B to overcome these negatives and must also stress its mellow, smooth taste. Tone must be glamorous, up-market and in keeping with after-dinner (rather than in-pub) brandy drinking.

Indigestion Remedy C:
Due to its polymethylsiloxane ingredient C is an especially effective treatment for wind and 'bloating' symptoms of indigestion and must be promoted specifically for regular sufferers from these symptoms. No other treatment is currently being promoted on this platform. Research shows indigestion sufferers to be highly conscious of these problems, and to be seeking a new, scientific solution.

A Word on USPs

One of the best known, but unfortunately most misused, ways of defining a creative strategy is the Unique Sales Proposition, or USP. (Note that USP does not stand for Unique Sales Point as is frequently and incorrectly claimed.) The concept of the USP was originated as long ago as the 1940s by Ted Bates and Company, an American agency and one of the world's largest. It was made famous in the 1960s by Rosser Reeves, then Chairman of Ted Bates, who published it in a seminal bestselling book called *Reality in Advertising*.* Reeves defined USP in three parts:

1. Each advertisement must make a proposition to the consumer. Not just words, not just product puffery, not just show-window advertising. Each advertisement must say to each reader: Buy *this* product and you will get *this* specific benefit.
2. The proposition must be one that the competition either cannot, or does not, offer. It must be unique—either a uniqueness of the brand or a claim not otherwise made in that particular field of advertising.
3. The proposition must be so strong that it can move the mass millions i.e. pull over new customers to your product.

These three parts of the USP definition are worth studying carefully, since they encapsulate most of the underlying thinking that must go into all effective creative strategies, no matter in what form they are written. Nevertheless in the years since Reeves first published his book the USP approach has been frequently attacked, on several grounds:

1. It applies only to mass market branded goods, which as we have seen account for but 40 % or so of total advertising.
2. It is biased too strongly towards the copy rather than *art*

---

* *Reality and Advertising* is now out of print, but is well worth reading if you can get hold of a copy. (See Bibliography) content of advertisements; it is difficult to verbalise the proposition implicit in an illustration.

3. As a consequence, it tends to emphasise the *logical* reasons for buying products and minimise the purely *emotional* reasons.

4. Finally, and most fundamentally, it is circular in form—since it defines a 'selling proposition' as one that will 'pull over new customers' i.e. as one that will sell!

Each of these criticisms has some justice. Nevertheless the discipline implicit in the USP theory can be exceptionally helpful when you are trying to disentangle the woolly nuances often involved in the formulation of creative strategy.

How should the advertisements say it?

In reality, when a campaign is being created, this section on creative techniques occurs simultaneously with the next section—*Creating the advertisements*. Experienced copywriters and art directors, when devising advertisements, will automatically keep in mind the techniques available and choose those most suitable for the product under consideration.

What do we mean here by creative techniques? Simply the verbal and visual form in which the final advertisement will appear. The basic forms available, and the choices which have to be made are:

Press and magazines	Long or short copy?
	Illustration—colour or black and white?
	Photography, drawing or design?
	Product or people?
Headlines	Explanatory or 'teaser'?
Television and cinema	Photography or cartoon?
	Real life or fantasy?
	Presenter or product demonstration?

Radio	Presenter, jingle or scenario?
Posters	Photography, drawing or design?
Direct Mail	Letters, leaflets or gimmicks?

Let us now look in detail at what the different techniques are, and at how they are used. In every case the reasons for using one technique, or combination of techniques, rather than another will be complex, and a large number of important books have been written which cover the techniques individually. Here we must take an overall view of the basic *principles* involved in selecting the right creative technique for each situation.

Press and magazines

Long or short copy?—The general rule is that people are willing and even anxious to read more about expensive goods, less about cheap ones. You will want to know a great deal more before you buy a car than before you buy a lollipop.

Illustrations—As we have noted, the use of colour is especially desirable for fashion, cosmetics and food; for other fields black and white will suffice, though it should be noted that colour always increases readership and impact. Drawings are best used where humour or fantasy are required; they are also generally less expensive than photographs and reproduce better on poor paper. Photographs are more realistic, more involving and easier for the reader to identify with. Pure design, without illustration, is used mostly for services and 'intangibles'. Unillustrated design advertisements are not found frequently today because photography and drawings are known to increase readership and impact.

Larger advertisements will almost always include illustrations both of people (using the product) and the product itself (pack shot). In smaller advertisements a choice between them may need to be made. If the pack is new or unknown it should be displayed prominently. Including people in an advertisement will increase reader involvement and impact.

Headlines—Many leading advertising practitioners believe that headlines should always be self-explanatory and never 'tease'. (Because on average only about half of those who see a headline bother to read the copy.) However, there are occasions when 'teaser' headlines have a role, usually as part of a very heavy campaign or to interest readers in an intrinsically uninteresting product. But as a general rule, use teasers rarely and circumspectly.

Television and Cinema

Photography or cartoon?—As in press advertising, cartoons are best used when humour or fantasy are required; they are also often used when a photograph might be indelicate or tasteless (e.g. for denture cleansers). They are generally more expensive than photography. As before, photography is more realistic, more involving and easier to identify with.

Real life or fantasy?—Fantasy is sometimes portrayed photo-graphically. This is done deliberately to make the fantasy seem more realistic and believable (even though both advertiser and public are well aware that it *is* fantasy!). This technique is usually highly expensive, but can achieve great glamour and/or romance.

Presenter or product demonstration?—For complicated product stories, or where several items or messages must be put across, it is often best to use a 'presenter' (a man or woman talking straight to camera). Famous personalities often add extra interest and credibility. For technically complicated products, or products which achieve immediately visible effects, before-and-after demonstrations of how they work are usually the best way to sell them.

Radio

Presenter, jingle, or scenario?—Effective use of the radio medium requires a high level of repetition for the advertisement to be memorable. Also, because only sound is involved messages must be kept especially simple. Presenters should be used, as with television, for complicated stories. Jingles are ideal for light-hearted, inexpensive purchases, such as ice-cream and confectionery. A scenario, or playlet, can add realism and credibility where these are felt to be particularly necessary.

Posters

Photography, drawing or design?—Because posters are mostly seen by people who are moving (in buses, trains, cars or on foot) the message must again be kept extremely simple, and brief. The guidelines for when to use photography, drawings or design are the same as for the press; *but* photographs must be extremely simple and uncluttered, and simple graphic design is frequently the clearest way to communicate in this medium.

Direct Mail

Letters, leaflets or gimmicks?—In direct mail the cost of production is usually an important element in deciding which techniques should be used. A duplicated letter is far and away the cheapest form of direct mail; printed leaflets are considerably more expensive; and gimmicks are almost always the most costly. Letters, although sometimes despised as being an unimaginative approach, can generate good results if their message is interesting and succinct. And great care must be taken in the selection of gimmicks: they are often seen by recipients to be extravagant and irritatingly wasteful.

Having chosen which technique or combination of techniques, should be used, the advertisement can now be created.

Creating the advertisements

All creative processes are difficult to describe, and the creation of advertisements is no exception. Throughout the ages many writers, artists and musicians have endeavoured to set down the way they are inspired to work; but despite their efforts the answers elude them. All that can be said with certainty is that to achieve success both natural talent *and* blood, sweat and tears will be called for. As Thomas Edison, the famous American scientist and inventor, put it, 'Genius is 1 % inspiration and 99 perspiration'.

With regard to advertising the blood, sweat and tears will involve acquiring a fundamental knowledge of the product or service in question: trying it, trying its competitors studying all the available research, talking to ordinary people who use it, discussing it with people in the agency. To do all these things thoughtfully and enthusiastically requires time and energy and dedication: it is easy to be tempted to cut corners, but disastrous to do so.

Having done the basic research the copywriter and art director then sit down together and work to develop the basic *concept* for the advertisement. *Concept* is the terminology used for the underlying idea or theme of the advertisement. Not all advertisements have an idea or theme—but they all should. An idea will capture the interest of a prospective customer as no mere statement of facts will. But first and foremost *the concept must be relevant to the product* and interpret precisely the creative strategy. To return to our earlier literary analogy: the form (concept) must precisely convey the content (strategy).

This is a most important point, and difficult to grasp in practice. Because of the nebulous nature of concepts and ideas it is often unclear whether or not they are 'on strategy'. An unusual and striking concept will inevitably tend to seduce everybody into wanting to believe it is on strategy, even if it is not quite right. Bill Bernbach, a founder of Doyle, Dane, Bernbach, one of the world's greatest creative agencies, has said that it is easy to get attention; all you need to do is show a child walking upside down on his hands

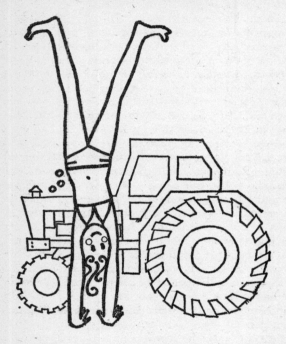

along the middle of Broadway—but it would not be *relevant* unless you were advertising a product which stopped coins falling out of trouser pockets!

The apocryphal industrial advertiser's answer to all creative problems—'Put a pretty girl on the tractor'—would be good, effective advertising if the tractor had been especially designed to be driven by pretty girls. However, seeking attention at all costs, even irrelevantly, is a danger on only one side of the creative coin. The reverse side involves saying the right thing so overtly or so boringly that nobody will bother to look at the advertisement. And deciding in advance whether or not an advertisement will be uninteresting may be even more difficult than judging whether it is on strategy.

This may seem surprising, since we all like to think we instinctively know what will and will not be interesting to our fellow men. Unfortunately we rarely find ourselves advertising to our fellow men. The target market may be young mothers, or elderly budgie-owners, or advokaat drinkers or farmers. Having done some thorough basic research, we will have a fairly good idea of what they are looking for from the product; but it will still be hard to judge whether or not the message is being conveyed in a way that is striking and interesting *to them*. This is one of the commonest faults made by amateur commentators on advertising; and it is frequently made by professionals in client and agency organisations too. When creating an advertisement it is vital to try to put yourself, so far as possible, into the mind of the true prospective customer. And if you are not a young mother or an elderly budgie-owner, if you hate advokaat or have never so much as visited a farm, this will not be a simple thing for you to do. Nevertheless good agency creative people must teach themselves to do it.

The copywriter and art director, then, must dream up a concept that is relevant *and* striking for the target market. Today it is common for copywriters and art directors to do this literally *together*, working in the same room, throwing ideas at each other, arguing and striking sparks off each other, scribbling out rough concepts and rejecting them until they are reasonably certain that they have licked the problem. However, it used to be more common for copywriters and art directors to work separately, and the practice still persists in some agencies. Where this system pertains it is almost invariably the copywriter who originates the basic concept, and then gives it to the art director to *visualise*.

Whichever way the work is done, the end result will be the same. A *rough* or *scamp* will be produced. The *rough* will usually be a loose drawing made by the art director, indicating what the final photo or illustration will be, and hand-lettering the headline and product name. All other wording will be indicated by squiggled lines, which are merely intended to show where the words will be placed and approximately how much space they will occupy. This *rough* or *scamp* is produced in order to show the executives within the agency and also of course the client what the advertisement will be like. As you can imagine, interpreting a *rough* requires some experience on the part of the viewer; and occasionally differences of opinion occur at a later stage when it transpires that the client and the art director visualised the end product in different ways.

To minimise such disagreements the agency may sometimes produce *finished roughs*. These will show a much more finished drawing depicting the illustration or photograph, together with a printed headline. Obviously *finished roughs* cost much more to produce than ordinary *roughs* or *scamps*, and so agencies try to avoid them. However, for clients with little experience of advertising—and these can include the chairmen of large companies as well as raw trainee recruits —the production of *finished roughs* may be unavoidable.

Roughs are used for all press and magazine advertisements and for direct mail and below-the-line promotions. For television and cinema commercials, *scripts* and/or *storyboards* are produced. The function of a storyboard is exactly the same as that of a rough. It indicates what the final commercial will be, so that the client can consider and approve it before money is spent on its production. A *storyboard* comprises a number of drawn 'stills' in sequence, which give a very approximate idea of what the commercial will look like; and beneath each 'still' will be written the camera instructions and the sound that will be used simultaneously. As with press roughs, *storyboards* can either be loosely scamped or highly finished, depending on the requirements of the client.

Whether finished or scamped, storyboards are quite expensive to draw up, and some agencies now make a separate charge for them to their clients. To avoid this cost, *scripts* may be produced instead of storyboards. This is particularly common if the agency has several possible approaches which it wishes to discuss with the client prior to developing one of them into a final recommendation. Scripts break down into video (vision) and audio (sound), and look like this:

Client: Purple and Mauve Manufacturing Company
Product: Newly-designed 'Relaxez-Vous' Armchair
Commercial title: 'Big Man' (*30 seconds*)

Video	Audio
1. Long shot of spotlit Relaxez-Vous armchair from behind, dark limbo setting.	1. 1½ seconds silence.
2. Camera tracks-in quickly. It is seen that pipe smoke is rising above chair.	2. Music starts suddenly. Double-bass plucked at speed, excitingly.
3. Chair swings round. In it is sitting a huge man, tall, broad. (30s; handsome, casually dressed, smoking pipe). He speaks to camera.	3. Music dies down to gentle background behind voice. Man speaks 'When it comes to armchairs, I'm not a very easy chap to suit . . .'
4. Cut to same man in ordinary armchair, patently uncomfortable, grimacing.	4. '. . . because most of the things seem to have been designed for tiny people . . .'
5. Cut again to man in another armchair, leaning forward to close-up to camera.	5. '. . . with curved backs . . .'
6. Cut again to man in another armchair with long base, his legs sticking out uncomfortably.	6. '. . . or quite extraordinarily long thighs . . .'
7. Fast dissolve back to Relaxez-Vous chair. Man taps out pipe in ashtray resting easily on chair arm, crosses his legs comfortably.	7. 'Now Purple and Mauve have designed a chair that's comfortable however big you are, or however small you are, and whatever shape you are . . .'
8. Man leans his head to one side and his eyes droop, then close. He is asleep.	8. '. . . The only thing I have against it is it's far too . . ssszz.'

Video	Audio
9. Super Title: 'Relaxez-Vous Armchair' The trouble is it's far too ... ssszz. ...	9. Music fades up again, now gently. Ends softly but suddenly. ½-second silence.

(*Note:* All television commercials in the U.K. must start with 1½ seconds silence and end with ½ second silence to avoid succeeding commercials clashing with each other).

If this script were to be 'storyboarded', there would be nine or ten drawings illustrating each of the *video* situations, with the camera directions and *audio* written under each of them.

Finally, radio commercials are always produced in script form, but as most agencies have a tape or cassette recorder, often they will make an amateur in-house tape to give the client a rough idea of what the end result will sound like.

Executing the advertisements

When the advertisement idea has been created and approved by the client, it must be transformed to the final stage to be ready for printing or transmission. How this is done will obviously vary, depending upon the medium in which the advertisement is to appear. But whichever medium is being used, the initial two stages will be the same.

(*i*) Selection of a specialist to execute the idea.
(*ii*) Briefing the specialist.

(*i*) *Selection.* The creative work that has been done so far will all have been carried out *within* the advertising agency. The creation of ideas, you will remember, is one of the functions that agencies carry out free, within their commission payments. Contrary to what most outsiders believe, however, photographs, drawings, filming and typesetting are almost never carried out within agencies but are done by independent suppliers.

There are three reasons for this. First, agencies could not afford to supply these services free of charge and therefore would need to charge additionally for them even if they did them themselves. Second, and more important, the production of these items is intensely specialised: a good fashion artist is unlikely to be good at drawing portraits, the best food photographers are rarely as good at action shots, and film directors who are marvellous at handling actors may know virtually nothing about cartoon animation. Third, the most talented of such people tend to be independent, not to say temperamental, spirits who prefer to work alone and outside organisations.

It is the job of the agency to select the right horse for each course. Usually this will be done by the copywriter and art director who produced the concept. They will recommend the person or persons whom they believe will execute their ideas best. This recommendation will then need to be agreed by those in the agency working on the account, and sometimes by the client as well. In order to be sure that they have picked the best possible horse, copywriters and art directors need to keep themselves closely in touch with all the photographers, artists and film directors available. This is a vital and time-consuming aspect of their job. In the largest agencies they will be aided in making their selections by an *art-buyer*, who will be a full-time employee of the agency, and whose specialised job it will be to keep abreast of all the talent available.

Having chosen the person to do the job, the agency art director will then need to select actors and models, props, maybe a set designer, and possibly a home economist or a fashion advisor. These people will be selected in co-operation with the photographer or film director. It would be foolish for the art director to choose, for example, an actor that the film director considered quite wrong for the part or simply could not get on with. These selections may also need to be approved within the agency and by the client—particularly the actors/models, about whom clients frequently have strong views.

One of the most important factors in this selection process

is the one that has not yet even been mentioned: money. There is a very wide range of charges and costs in this area, and the best talents (or at least those most highly in demand) can charge what seem to many outsiders to be quite exorbitant fees for their services.

A budget should always be fixed to cover the cost of executing the advertisements well in advance—even before the copywriter and art director start work on producing concepts. There can be little point in them producing a concept that needs to be shot in, for example, the Himalayas if the execution budget only runs to a few hundred pounds; likewise there is no point in considering the use of Bob Hope or Sophia Loren if the budget is very tight. Right from the beginning the concept must be produced within financial constraints.

These financial constraints will come into force directly in the selection of the photographer, artist or film director. To give you some idea of the costs involved, here are the fees which might be charged by the cheapest and most expensive talents:

	Colour Photography	Line Drawing	30-second Commercial
Lowest price	£20	£5	£3,000
Top price	£1,000	£500	£30,000

Now it is incorrect to imply that it is only the fee for the photographer etc. which controls these charges. Obviously the complexity and intrinsic cost of the job will also be extremely important. Trips to the Himalayas and lavishly built sets are more expensive than pictures that can be shot in a bare studio around the corner. The set for the Purple and Mauve 'Relaxez-Vous' commercial would have been cheap, but it would have been very important to obtain a first-class actor and a subtle director to avoid being heavy-handed and gauche. As a concrete example, that particular commercial would cost anything between £3,000 and £10,000 depending upon casting and direction.

Obviously, this is a very delicate area in the relationship between agency and client. Most clients suspect that agencies are somewhat spendthrift in the money they spend on the execution of advertisements. The Purple and Mauve Finance Director would find it exceptionally difficult to comprehend why he should be asked to provide £10,000 for a commercial that could be made for £3,000. 'Will this nicer, subtler commercial,' he will be tempted to ask, 'sell sufficient extra armchairs to generate the extra £7,000 it will cost? Or will the general public not even notice the difference?' It is not an easy question to answer. All that can be said is that over the years the leading advertisers have generally come to believe it to be worthwhile to pay the higher prices charged by the leading talent. After all, if the Relaxez-Vous commercial is going out on national television, £300,000 or more may be spent on showing it. Surely in these circumstances it cannot be worth risking spoiling the ship for a ha'porth of tar?

(*ii*) *Briefing*. It is necessary here to dwell for a moment on the important subject of *briefing*.

Having selected the people who will execute and produce the advertisement it is essential that a really thorough briefing should be given to them. Some agencies, and some clients, insist that these briefings should be written down and agreed in advance. Generally speaking, however, it is left to the art director to give the briefing in his own words and in his own way. Whichever way the matter is handled, the more deeply the photographer or artist understands what is required of him, and understands the *reasons* why the job is being done in the way that it is, the more likely it is that the end result will be exactly right. Remember the costs involved in taking photographs and making commercials and you will immediately realise how important it is that these things should be done correctly the first time.

To be done properly, the briefing will take some time and may involve several meetings. Initially the original rough or storyboard or scripts will be shown, and the person whose job it will be to execute the advertisements will ask questions; either there and then or shortly afterwards a price will be quoted. (In the case of television commercials the price may take some time to estimate.) In the ensuing days further questions will occur as *every detail* is considered and resolved. Nothing should be left to chance. What colour should the model's hair be? What should she be wearing? How exactly should she be sitting, or standing, or moving? And so on. All of these minuscule incidentals may influence, even if unconsciously, the final viewer of the advertisement. Therefore they must be thought out carefully, and if something cannot be resolved within the agency it should be referred back to the client.

Then at last, when all the briefings and preparation have been completed, the photograph can be taken, or the commercial can be shot. The art director must always be present on the day to answer and decide upon any last-minute queries. The copywriter will wish to be there too if he has the time, as he has generally been responsible for the creation of about half the advertisement. And on any important shoot the client, accompanied by the agency client contact executive, will almost certainly be present. It is his money that is being spent and he will want to ensure that it is being spent well!

Trade Unions

All commercials, and certain artwork, must be produced by union houses. In the case of commercials, films not made by members of the Association of Cinematograph and Television Technicians Union will be blacked by members of the staff of the television companies. In the U.S.A. the American Federation of Television and Radio Artists (AFTRA) is similarly involved in the making of all television and radio commercials.

In the case of press advertising the situation is more

complex because several trade unions operate and overlap membership, but to an ever-increasing extent it is becoming necessary for producers of artwork to be union members, to prevent advertisements from being blacked by members of the printing staff on the newspapers. To a certain extent, particularly in the case of television commercials, it is the trade unions' requirements which influence costs.

Producing the advertisements

We have now reached the final phase in the making of an advertisement, the production stage. Together with media selection, production is one of the most technical aspects of advertising, and considerable knowledge is required to master it fully. Predictably, it is necessary to consider production for the various media separately. The production stages involved in each are as follows:

> *Press and magazines*
>   (*a*) choice of typography
>   (*b*) choice of method of typesetting: metal or film
>   (*c*) choice of printing process: letterpress, litho or
>   gravure; black/white or colour.
> *Television and Cinema:* choice of film or videotape?
> *Posters:* choice of printing processes: litho or silk-screen?
> *Radio:* tape production.

Press and magazines

(*a*) *Typography*—*Typography* lies on the borderline between *executing* the advertisement and *producing* it. Typography is the job of specifying the size and style of typematter to be used. The size of type is measured in *points* and *ems*, a system first invented in the United States in the eighteenth century. A point is a seventy-second of an inch and there are twelve points to the *em* (or *pica em*) which thus equals one-sixth of an inch. The style of the type is called the *typeface* and nowadays there are literally thousands of typefaces to choose from. Here are six:

Clarendon   **Egyptian**   Scotch Roman

Klang   Times New Roman   Univers

Each *typeface* will exist in several forms which match together:

lower case   UPPER CASE   *Italic*

Light   **Bold**   **Condensed**

The *typographer* produces a precisely detailed drawing of the typematter to be used, which is called the *type spec* (or type mark-up). This is sent to the *typesetters* who make up the type exactly as the typographer wants it, reproduce the type on paper and return copies of this printed sheet (proofs) to the typographer for checking.

It should be mentioned here that the *typographer*, like the other *executors* of the advertisements mentioned in the last section, works under the guidance of the art director. Typographers sometimes work within agencies, sometimes they freelance. The best are fine craftsmen, who by use of their skill can turn even a dully designed advertisement into an attractive and easily readable one.

(*b*) *Typesetting*—The simplest way to understand what *typesetters* do is to think of them as printers who do not do the final printing. They set type for the trade, rather than for the public. They carry hundreds of different typefaces, each in all of its sizes and styles. Traditionally these faces are kept as individual metal pieces in large trays. The *typesetter* picks the letters from the tray one by one, as specified by the typographer on the *type spec*. This is called *hand-setting* and is of course a highly skilled craft.

A quicker and more advanced form of typesetting is *machine-setting*. This is done with a typewriter-like machine, which the typesetter uses in much the same way as a secretary. But instead of typewriter-ribbon the keys release moulds on to molten metal, thus forming the letter shapes as the metal is speedily cooled and solidifies. This form of type-setting offers fewer varieties of typeface than handsetting, and also offers less control of the space between individual letters and words. It is far cheaper, however, and is there-fore still used extensively for advertisements with large amounts of copy, such as those for unit trusts.

Much the most modern form of typesetting is *photosetting*, which is now used very widely in the United States and to an ever-increasing extent throughout Europe. In photo-setting the complete typeface in all its varieties (but in only one basic size) exists on a piece of film just like a photo-graphic negative. To produce typesetting the film is placed in a machine similar to a photographic enlarger which projects the letters on the film individually on to light-sensitive paper. The typesetter spells words by selecting the letters in order, and has complete flexibility of typesize and of spacing between letters and words. It is the development of *photosetting* which has brought so many new typefaces into existence, since all that is needed for a complete face is a piece of film rather than a costly set of metallic letters or moulds.

(c) *Printing processes*—The form in which the final material is prepared for the newspaper or magazine will depend upon the printing process used by the publication. All publications are today printed by one of three processes:

Letterpress
Litho (lithography)
Gravure (photogravure)

Each process can be used to print both black/white and colour. *Letterpress* is still the most common method used for printing publications, particularly newspapers. The great majority of national and local newspapers in Britain and throughout the world are printed letterpress because of its versatility and flexibility.

Letterpress printing works by *raising* the area to be

printed (or in practice cutting back the area not to be printed), then coating the raised area with ink and pressing it against the paper. If you have ever done any potato printing, or if you used a John Bull Printing Kit when you were a child, then you were effectively using the letterpress principle. It is the oldest form of printing, as invented by William Caxton, and in a highly mechanised form it is still generally the cheapest method for straightforward black and white type.

Photographs are printed letterpress by translating them into a dot pattern; large dots pick up more ink and print darker, small dots print lighter. The number of dots to the inch (2·5 cm) is called the *screen* of the printing. National and local newspapers, which use fairly rough paper, must use quite a coarse screen, usually 65. Magazines especially glossies, can use much finer screens, up to 133. The coarser the screen the less detailed the quality of reproduction of the original picture; the finer, the more detailed the final result will be.

Colour letterpress printing in publications works by printing four standard inks—red, yellow, blue and black— one on top of the other and blending the dots so that the eye sees the colour being reproduced. However, it is most important to realise, both for letterpress and for the other printing techniques described below, that colour printing in mass-circulation publications cannot be perfect. First, because the colour is achieved with the use of four standard inks only a limited range of hues (running into hundreds none the less) can be reproduced. More subtle hues can be printed with more inks, or with specially mixed inks, but publications cannot afford to print advertisements in this way. Second, the finest quality printing is a slow, craft business, whereas mass publications must be printed on fast-running machines. Third, different advertisements and editorial which are printed close to each other will slightly affect each other's colour.

Experienced, professional art directors and photographers

keep all these technical qualifications in mind from the start and do not try to make the publications print material beyond the limit of their technical facilities. On the other hand, most art directors (and clients for that matter) believe that publications *could* achieve far better quality colour reproduction even within the economic and technical limitations inherent in their printing processes, if only they took more trouble. And the most conscientious publications strive continuously to improve their performance in this regard.

Litho (*lithography*) is becoming ever more popular for the printing of magazines and weekly newspapers. Its main virtue is that it prints a more acceptable quality of reproduction than letterpress on inexpensive paper, and that it uses a long-lasting printing plate which makes it economical for long print runs.

Litho printing is basically a photographic process, in which a coated metal plate is exposed (as if it were a film) to the image to be reproduced. The coating on the metal plate works on the principle that grease (printing ink) and water will not mix. After being photographically exposed it is damped and inked; the ink adheres only to the coated parts of the plate which carry the image. It is then absorbed from those same parts on to the paper to produce the final result. Litho is used to print fine screens from 120 to even 200 to the inch (2·5 cm); however, the plate-making and preparation are more difficult to alter and correct than is the case for letterpress, making the process somewhat less flexible.

The modern litho machine is *offset*, which means that the metal plate prints on to a rubber blanket which in turn offsets the image on to the paper. This minimises the wear on the metal plate so that it lasts longer. In the *web-offset-litho* process the paper is fed into the machine from a reel (the web) instead of from a flat bed of sheets, and this greatly increases printing speeds. As with letterpress, litho printing normally uses four standard inks so that only a limited number of colours can be reproduced.

Photogravure is different from both letterpress and litho in that the area to be printed is cut *into* the metal printing plate with acid. This process (traditionally called *intaglio*) is fundamentally the same as that used in etching except that for photogravure the cut does not go nearly so deeply into the metal. A spirit ink is used which is sucked out of the recessed areas by the paper, thus producing the image. The deeper the cut, the more ink will be held and the heavier will be the printing.

Photogravure is cheaper than either letterpress or litho for really long runs of publications where high quality is not absolutely vital. The British woman's weekly magazines—*Woman, Woman's Own* and *Woman's Weekly*—are all printed by photogravure and they give a fair representation of its abilities. Under a magnifying glass the edges of the letters on a page of photogravure are far more jagged than those off a letterpress printing plate—which is the result of the gravure process. The printing plates are huge rolls like rolls of lino, each roll printing a single colour, with four rolls printing in rapid succession one after the other. These huge printing plate rolls take even longer to prepare than litho plates; and having been prepared they are exceptionally costly and difficult to alter. Thus photogravure is the least versatile and flexible of the three processes we have discussed.

Artwork

Artwork is the technical name given to the final image from which the printer or platemaker reproduces. Artwork does not need to be a drawing, nor even a photograph. Hand-drawn lettering or even a page of type can be artwork if it is used to reproduce from. Apart from the printing process itself, the quality of the artwork is the factor which most determines the quality of the printed end result. The production of artwork for black and white reproduction is reasonably straightforward; the typesetter produces the artwork of the wording and the artist or photographer produces the illustration artwork (retouched if necessary).

A *tracing guide*—literally a tracing—shows the printer how these separate pieces of artwork are to be positioned together in the final advertisement. When the separate pieces have been positioned together the complete artwork is often called a *mechanical*.

The production of colour artwork is altogether more complicated—though at its simplest it merely involves the use of an original colour transparency, taken by the photographer. Printing can be carried out directly from photographic transparencies. Indeed if these have been perfectly exposed they deliver the highest possible quality of colour reproduction. Frequently, however, it is not possible to reproduce straight from the transparency. Complex retouching may be needed, or the colour balance may need changing—and only the simplest of alterations can be effected on an original colour transparency. An expensive colour print, known as a *dye-transfer* will then need to be made, on which the retoucher can work; and the printer will reproduce from the *dye-transfer*. Unfortunately this process of transferring transparency to dye-transfer to printer almost inevitably involves a loss of quality unless the most stringent care is taken.

In the case of photogravure publications, the advertising agency supplies artwork to the journal's printer and he makes the plates normally without further charge. (The cost is in fact built into the media's charge for space.) For litho publications, the agency generally has litho films made and sends these, rather than artwork, to the publication. Lastly, in the case of letterpress publications the agency makes the plates, using an outside plate-making house, and charges the client for them. The cost of letterpress colour plates can be high, as much as £500 per set, and this factor can deter clients from taking colour advertising in letterpress printed magazines.

Television and Cinema

Film and videotape. Videotape can be used only on television. Under present and foreseeable cinema projection facilities, commercials for this medium have to be made on film (though it is technically feasible to project videotape on to a big screen with quite satisfactory results).

We all know fairly well what movie film is and how it works. Videotape is pulsed magnetic tape which looks and functions just like sound tape, but produces vision (as well as sound). It is used extensively by the television broadcasting companies themselves, who very rarely use film. It is almost invariably cheaper than film, and invariably quicker to produce than film, since it requires no chemical processing and can be replayed instantly. All those *Action Replays* on television are in fact videotape recordings quickly run back and re-transmitted.

Videotape thus has many advantages over film, but also has several disadvantages:

1. Videotape equipment is cumbersome, expensive and far less mobile than film equipment.
2. Special effects—fades, dissolves, jumping lettering—cannot be done nearly so well on videotape.
3. It is similarly impractical for cartoon use.
4. The colour and picture qualities of videotape are less good than those of film.

As in any situation where alternative techniques exist for doing basically similar jobs, supporters of each polarise and tend to become excessively biased in favour of the approach they prefer to use. Suffice it to say here that the great majority of television commercials are still shot on film, but videotape is being used to an ever-increasing extent.

Whether or not the *final* commercial is shot on videotape, because of its cheapness and speedy flexibility tape is nowadays frequently used for two particular purposes:

(*a*) For casting, being unquestionably a great improvement on the static model photograph traditionally used for casting purposes.

(*b*) For rough commercials to be researched prior to being made in finished form (this subject will be dealt with in greater detail in the next chapter).

Posters

Printing processes: litho or silk-screen? Some posters, especially those on the large bulletin boards and supersites, are hand-painted, as you may have noticed. The great majority, though, are printed in small sections on paper and pasted together using either the lithography process described above—which is economical for large poster campaigns with long printing runs; or using silk-screen printing. Silk-screen printing is simply an advanced form of stencilling. Traditionally the stencil was made of silk (hence silk-screen) but today synthetic materials are used.

Silk-screen is frequently the cheapest method of printing small runs. Department stores, for example, mostly use silk-screen for their window bills. However, even the modern synthetic screens wear out quite quickly and the process can become slow and expensive for long runs; and the definition produced at the edges is less sharp than that achieved with lithography. Silk-screen is not ideally suitable for intricate illustrations nor for full-colour printing which necessitates the exact superimposition of layers of various coloured inks.

Radio

Tape production. Radio advertising was once described to me by the then head of Air Edel, one of the leading companies in the field of radio commercial production, as 'The most satisfying of all the advertising media to work in.' I was surprised, because most people prefer to work in glamorous television or to produce colour photography for glossy magazine advertisements; obviously I asked 'Why?' 'Because it is so instantaneous' was the reply. 'You work for a morning on a session, recording the tape. And it's made. No more trouble. You send it to the radio stations and the next thing you know, it's on air.'

This is true, by and large. Videotape is almost as instant, but almost always requires some amendment after completion. Whereas if the client is present at the recording session, radio can be approved for transmission on the spot.

In principle all that you need to make a radio commercial is your own tape recorder. However, unless your recording equipment is exceptionally fine, the end result would not sound too good when broadcast. And obviously you could not add sound effects and mix voices. But such things can be done quickly, easily and above all *inexpensively* in a professional sound recording studio, which is one reason why radio is an attractive medium for the small advertiser and the local advertiser, without a big budget and without much advertising expertise.

Who does what?

During the course of this chapter it has sometimes been necessary to sketch in the people responsible for the various stages in the procedure. Before closing the chapter it is necessary to pinpoint these responsibilities more precisely. The demarcation lines cannot be hard and fast. In advertising even more than in most other activities people become involved in other people's jobs, as has already been said. Nevertheless for the complicated task of producing an advertising campaign to be carried out efficiently, individuals need to be made responsible for the successive stages in the process. Here are the designations of the people who will do each of the jobs of work, which will then be approved and authorised by senior management in both the agency and the client company.

Stage	Client personnel	Agency personnel	Outside Supplier
A. Setting the objectives	Marketing director Marketing manager Advertising manager Brand manager	Account director Account team	
B. How much should be spent?	Marketing manager Advertising manager Brand manager	Account director Account team Media	
C. Where should it be spent?		Account team Media	
D. What should the advertisements say?	Marketing mgr. Advertising mgr. Brand mgr.	Account dir. Account team Creative	
E. How should they say it?		Creative Production	
F. Creating the advertisements		Creative	
G. Executing the advertisements		Creative Production	Photographers, artists Film production etc.
H. Producing the advertisements		Account team Creative Production	Typographers, typesetting Blockmakers, printers etc.

Throughout the process the agency account director and members of the client company will be continuously involved in discussions, suggestions and approvals—until the final proof or television commercial appears and the true arbiters, the prospective customers, make their own, all-important decision.

Think Exercises

1. A leading manufacturer of washing machines will be visiting your agency with a view to asking you to plan a campaign for him. Think of a dozen questions you will want to ask him when he comes, to which you will require answers before the campaign can be formulated.

2. Study the current advertising for Coca-Cola, Ford cars and Lux soap, and try to define exactly what their creative strategies are.

3. Your best friend has invented a golf ball which flies further with less effort. Together you decide to manufacture and market it. You scrape together a few thousand pounds between you, and your bank manager generously agrees to back the venture with a modest overdraft. Your role is to plan the launch campaign. You will not be able to afford to employ experts so you will have to do this job yourself from beginning to end. Draw up a plan.

6

Does It All Work?

'I know that half of the money I spend on advertising is wasted,' the late Lord Leverhulme, founder of the great Unilever Empire, is often quoted as saying, 'but I have no means of knowing which half.' Were he alive today, with the aid of modern market research techniques he could probably at least reduce the wasted half to a wasted one-third. But apart from direct response advertising (which we have already discussed in detail) even today no research techniques exist which can guarantee the effectiveness of every advertisement. Market research in advertising is a matter of *odds*: used skilfully it increases the *odds* on success, decreases the *odds* on failure.

What is market research?

Market research comprises drawing a *representative sample* of the population and finding out what kind of people they are, how they behave, what they believe and how they are likely to behave in the future. It is essentially *predictive*; there is rarely any commercial purpose in finding out about people's past behaviour except in so far as it helps you to predict their future behaviour. The predictions are, however, not as reliably accurate as those in, for example, physics, and as a result there is much debate as to whether market research is or is not a science.

The words *population* and *representative sample* have particular technical meanings in market research: *population* (sometimes called *universe*) is the totality of the group of people being studied. It may or may not mean the entire population of the country; it may mean the population of a region or a town; it may mean everyone under 35, or all car owners, or all whisky drinkers. In advertising the market research *population* is usually the *target market*.

A *representative sample* comprises a small proportion of the population whose habits and attitudes accurately reflect those of the population with a high degree of mathematical certainty (generally 95% or 19 to 1 is considered to be the minimum acceptable certainty).

In principle, of course, it is always possible to research the entire population. This is what really happens at General Elections, Referenda and in a Census. However, discovering an entire population's activities and views is normally prohibitively costly. By drawing a *representative sample* from a *population*, market research makes it possible to find out about that population at an acceptable cost.

Everybody knows about the well-publicised failings of opinion polls prior to certain of the British general and American presidential elections. In the light of the definitions given above, you will now realise that inaccurate predictions are bound to occur sometimes in market research. The professional researcher must seek to minimise the likelihood of such inaccuracies, and to do this within the constraints of cost. The three main areas where errors can creep in are

> Sampling
> Questioning
> Human Changeability

Let us look at how the market researcher deals with them.

Sampling techniques

To understand sampling fully requires a knowledge of advanced mathematics. The subject, based on statistics, is highly technical, though several of the books on market research listed in the bibliography explain it clearly. Fortunately all that is required from the point of view of learning about advertising research is to know about the two main *sampling techniques*, and the advantages and disadvantages of each of them.

1. Random Sampling—mathematically this is the purest and most reliable method of sampling; unfortunately it is also much the most expensive. Random sampling involves going through the population and selecting each 100th or each 200th person completely at random, usually from the Electoral Roll. These people, and no others, are then interviewed. The reason that random sampling is so costly is that it is difficult and time-consuming to carry out. It involves interviewers in a great deal of travelling to find each selec-

ted member of the sample; and it may involve several calls in order to trace them.

A less expensive, though less pure, form of random sampling is *random walk* sampling. Here the interviewer starts at one address chosen at random. Having completed the interview there, the interviewer's instructions are to walk down the street, turning right or left whenever a dead end is reached, and conduct an interview at every 100th (or 200th etc. as necessary) address.

Should there be nobody in at one address, the interviewer simply walks on to the next 100th (or 200th) until the requisite number of interviews have been completed. It will be obvious that *random walk* sampling is quicker than pure *random* sampling, and therefore cheaper. However, it is less precise because the area chosen for the random walk may be atypical; and the kinds of people who are all out of their houses at the same time may also bias the results. (If there is a local Women's Institute meeting going on one afternoon unbeknown to the interviewer, most of the women of a particular type, age and class may well be attending it.)

2. Quota sampling—This is much the least expensive sampling technique, and much the most commonly used; but it is riddled with dangers of inaccuracy unless considerable care is taken. *Quota sampling* involves giving the interviewer a specified schedule showing the *quotas* of different sub-groups of the population from whom interviews must be obtained. For example if the interviewer needs to carry out fifty interviews the quota specification might be:

Male	Female	AB	C1	C2	DE
25	25	7	11	16	16

16-24	25-34	35-44	45+
12	12	12	14

The market research company carrying out the research would aim to ensure that interviews were carried out in an accurately representative sample of localities throughout the country. When all the interviewers had completed their work and sent in their questionnaires the company by totalling the interviews in the various sub-groups should obtain a balanced representative sample overall. For speed, and to keep costs down, quota sample interviews are often carried out in the street.

The dangers inherent in the quota sampling technique are:

1. Interviewer bias. Interviewers are only human, and will almost inevitably prefer to interview say, more respectable looking people, or older people not apparently in a hurry. Since it will not be possible for the research company to check on all the interviewees, the interviewer will be able to classify, for example, an over-45 as an under-45.

To avoid this, research companies seek to employ thoroughly experienced and reliable interviewers, and then to supervise them closely. Nevertheless interviewer bias is an ever-present problem in quota sampling.

2. On-street sampling skews the sample away from the people who rarely walk on the street, for example the aged and infirm, and the very rich.

3. Finally, quota sampling has a serious theoretical flaw. This is that the quotas can only be drawn up in terms of known (and easily defined) sub-groups—such as age, class, region, sex, brand usage etc. But what if the vital human characteristic influencing behaviour in a particular area is hair colour? Or height? Or ambition or political persuasion or colour blindness? The quota sample may comprise precisely the right number of ABs, 16–24s, and so on; but it may be (theoretically) that all of them have red hair, or are over 6ft tall, or are ambitious colour-blind Communists! Clearly such extreme biases are unlikely; however the possibility of such a bias occurring in quota sampling makes it mathematically less reliable than pure random sampling. (If the random sample has been correctly selected, the mathematical odds are that it will automatically contain the

right number of ambitious colour-blind Communists to be representative of the population at large!)

Framing questionnaires

A major problem relating to questionnaires is that it is easy to influence answers by the way in which questions are asked. Look at these questions, for example:

> 'If this excellent new product were on sale at an amazingly low price, would you buy it?'

Or,

> 'If there were an election tomorrow, would you vote for the present Government with its proven record of success, or would you risk gambling your vote on the opposition?'

Both these questions hint strongly at the replies they want to get. And they are only slightly exaggerated examples. In the 1950s, opinion polls were often carried out by politically motivated newspapers and the questions biased the results in precisely that kind of way. Such unprofessional practices reaped their own reward when the real election results proved the pollsters' forecasts to be nonsense. (And it is important to emphasise that no reputable market researcher would dream of using such loaded questions today.)

Nevertheless, even with the best and most ethical of intentions, the wording of questions can influence response. To minimise the possibility four rules should be followed:

1. Keep the object of the research, and particularly the brand or company in which you are primarily interested, 'hidden' from the respondent as far as possible. Once the respondent discovers that the interviewer is 'representing' Whipps Ice Cream, she will be prone to say things about Whipps that she does not really believe.

2. Keep emotive and value-judgement words out of the questions as far as possible. When you want to learn a

respondent's opinion, always offer opposites from which a choice can be made, so that the respondent cannot 'deduce' what you want the answer to be. Rating scales, discussed in the previous chapter, are usually the soundest way to tackle this problem.

3. Keep questions as factual and concrete as possible. 'Have you drunk Watney's beer in the last 12 months?' is a far better question than 'Have you ever drunk Watney's beer in your life?' Human memories are generally shorter and less reliable than we realise.

4. Keep questions free of difficult words and technical jargon. Remember that in most cases a proportion of respondents will have left school at 15 or even younger and may be only semi-literate. Using words that they do not understand —and it can often be a problem to avoid using such words— will both confuse and irritate them, leading them inexorably to give unreliable answers.

These are the basic rules. But the framing of questionnaires is really a technical job best left to experts. There are many additional pitfalls which can skew response, some of which are only now being discovered. (It has been shown, for example, that when responding to adjectival rating scales, people tend to prefer the adjectives at the top of a vertical list rather than those at the bottom.) The rules above are intended not so much to help you devise your own questionnaires, as to help you examine and judge whether a questionnaire has really been drawn up competently.

Human changeability

Advertising and market research would be much easier if human beings were not so unpredictable! Commercial market research being essentially predictive, it frequently falls foul of human beings' propensity to change their minds. (On the other hand, if you think deeply about it, if people never changed their minds at all, advertising and market research would be entirely redundant!)

What the market researcher must do is to take account of human changeability by being aware of the ways in which people are most likely, and least likely, to change. Attempts can also be made to separate those people who are most changeable in their habits from those who are least changeable. When launching a new product, for example, a company will need to know whether those who claim in pre-launch research that they will definitely try it are a fickle segment of the market, who will try anything and everything new. Such people can be identified by asking them about their previous buying habits.

Conversely, advertisers sometimes wish to identify those people most prone to change so that they can deliberately address their messages to them. This is the *opinion leader* or *'fashion leader'* theory. It is obvious that when the populace changes its tastes and buying habits—as for example from darker beers to lighter beers, or from plain to filter cigarettes—some people take to the new habit more quickly than others. The extent to which the later switchers follow the trend-setters as against the extent to which both groups merely react on different time-scales to the same external forces (for example, health scares used to promote filter cigarettes) has never been discovered. Doubtless it varies from market to market and from situation to situation. However, in the mid-1960s the opinion leader theory became very fashionable in advertising and market research, and many companies spent considerable sums of money in attempts to identify the opinion leaders. These efforts bore few rewards and usually produced little more than vague and unproductive generalisations. Nevertheless the concept of the 'opinion leader' is a real and important one. The Target Group Index (see p. 142) for instance, continues to define and analyse users of all products in three separate ways:

1. 'Those who on the whole prefer traditional things'
   'Those who prefer modern, up-to-date things'.

2. 'Those who prefer established products and brands'
   'Those who prefer new products and brands'.
3. 'Those who stick to established products and brands'
   'Those who like to try new products and brands'.

In other words, is the user basically conservative or basically adventurous?

Other areas of research

The introduction above relating to problems of sampling and questionnaire-framing is relevant to all aspects of market research. In this book we shall be concentrating on the use of market research for advertisement testing. However, before we focus on this single aspect of market research it is important to itemise briefly some of the other ways in which modern companies, and their advertising agencies use research in the development of their total marketing effort.

'Blind' product tests: representative samples of the target market are given the manufacturer's product and its leading competitors in unbranded but coded packages. The interviewer then obtains reactions to the various products, probing for different reactions to different attributes (i.e. one toilet soap may smell nicer, another may lather better, a third may last longer without going too soft, and so on). Finally the respondent is asked to make an overall choice between the products tested. A basic rule followed by most companies is not to launch a product that is not preferred to its leading competitors in a 'blind' test among a representative sample of the target market.

When 'blind' product tests are being carried out it is important in many instances to establish whether or not respondents can *genuinely* perceive differences between the products being tested or whether they are merely imagining or inventing differences, perhaps so as not to appear foolish to the interviewer. The most typical situation in, for ex-

ample, a taste test between two similar beers is for there to
be a percentage of respondents who *can* genuinely differentiate, while the rest cannot. If those unable to differentiate
constitute only a small minority of the respondents then they
can safely be ignored; the majority opinion will determine
the final result. But if it is likely that a high percentage of
respondents will not be able to differentiate but may *pretend*
they can, a blind 'triangle' test can be carried out in which
respondents are given three product samples (two of product A, one of product B) and asked to spot the odd man
out. Only those who can do so correctly are then used in the
real product test, since they have proven their ability to
distinguish genuinely between the products.

Packaging tests: here a representative of the target market
will be shown various new designs, usually clearly named as
being for the same product (otherwise their attitudes to the
different names may bias their reactions to the designs).
Again their reactions will be gauged on various attributes,
for example, colour, quality, style, lettering; and finally
they will be asked to make an overall preference choice. In
packaging tests it is dangerous to test new packs, for a new
product, against existing packs for existing and well-known
products. Respondents' prior attitudes to the existing brands
are certain to skew the response. Such tests can therefore
only be carried out if cautious pre-testing has been carried
out to eliminate the possibility of a misleading bias occurring.

Packaging tests sometimes use a *tachistoscope*. This is a
device somewhat like a 'What the butler saw' machine,
except that when you peer through the eyeholes you spy the
pack being tested, illuminated for a fraction of a second.
The duration of the illumination is extremely brief to start
with, and you are asked by the interviewer to describe
precisely what you saw. You then peer into the *tachistoscope*
again, the illumination is repeated for a longer period, and
the interviewer questions you again. The process continues,
with the illumination time continuously lengthening, until

you have clearly perceived and taken in the pack in detail. Then an alternative pack is placed in the *tachistoscope* and tested the same way; then another, and so on. The purpose of *tachistoscope* testing is to discover which of several packs will have the most instantaneous impact as the eye skims past them on the supermarket shelf.

Tachistoscopes are also used sometimes for advertisement testing, particularly in the case of posters, with exactly the same objective.

Name tests: these involve giving a representative sample of the target market a list of possible names for a new product and obtaining their 'off the cuff' reactions to each of them. Once again reactions on different attributes will be probed. Is the name glamorous or old-fashioned? Does it suggest energy? Vitality? Health? The attributes must be selected in such a way as to be relevant to the product in question. Finally overall preferences will as always be obtained.

Price tests: researching the most acceptable price level for a product is exceptionally difficult; indeed many people believe that it can rarely if ever be done with sufficient accuracy to be worthwhile. At first sight you might think that the problem would be simple enough to solve: you would allow a representative sample of the target market to use the product in the normal way and then ask either: '*How much would you be prepared to pay for this product if you saw it on sale in your usual shop?*' or '*If this product were on sale for 10p would you buy it?*'—increasing the price until the majority give a negative response.

In practice, both these methods are used but the results they deliver must always be treated with caution. The difficulties are:

(*i*) Some people quite deliberately underestimate what they will be prepared to pay because they hope in that way to influence the manufacturer to keep the price down.

(*ii*) Conversely, other people tend to say they will spend

more than they really will, because they are frightened of seeming poor to the interviewer.

(*iii*) Additionally, certain types of product encourage respondents in *research situations* to react quite differently from the way in which they react in real life. For example, mothers generally claim they will spend more on health products for their children, and less on cosmetics than they actually do once out shopping. No doubt the spirit is willing but the flesh is weak—a trait which makes price research very difficult.

Having made these qualifications, it is worth stating that many manufacturers do carry out price research, if only because a little information on consumers' attitudes to this important subject is better than none at all; if interpreted with care, the results obtained will provide guidance.

Advertisement testing

We have now tested the product, its packaging, its name and its price. If at any stage consumer testing had revealed unsatisfactory reactions to the item being tested, the project should immediately have been returned to the drawing board. The foolhardy optimism of going ahead with projects for which consumers have shown no liking is almost certain to end in disaster. (However, this is not to say that market research results must always be accepted without question and at their most naïve face value. As we have seen market research produces odds rather than certainties; it can give guidance, but can never make decisions.)

Confident that what we have to offer to the public is as good as we can make it, we are ready to start advertising. And the advertising, like all the other items in the mix, can be tested to check whether it is likely to be right. It can be tested at three stages:

1. Prior to commencement;
2. In an area;
3. During and after launch.

Tests at each stage can be useful but tests prior to the commencement of the campaign, when things can still easily be altered, are likely to be the most actionable and it is upon this stage of testing that we shall concentrate.

Pre-testing advertisements

You will remember from Chapter 5 that an advertisement goes through the following successive phases before final appearance:

1. Production of creative strategy;
2. Production of creative concept (press) or story-board (television);
3. Production of copy/artwork/proof (press) or commercial (television).

The advertisement can be tested in each or all of these phases.

However, it is important to note from the beginning two limitations to all forms of advertisement pre-testing. First, there is no known technique that can accurately measure the *persuasive* or *selling* power of an advertisement. Various techniques exist which attempt to approximate to this measurement; but in no case has a correlation between pre-test results and market-place sales achievement been verified. In most cases therefore pre-testing research aims to assess the indirect effects of advertisements—the effects which can be assessed reasonably accurately: interest, credibility, impact, comprehension, communication. All of these contribute to the selling power of an advertisement; but they are not, of course, the same thing.

Second, advertisement pre-testing techniques can only give *comparative* results. That is, if you test five variations you will discover which of the five is best—but you still may not know whether or not it is really any good. Even less will you know whether a sixth or seventh (or twentieth or hundredth) variation might not have been better still, however good the best of the original five turns out to be. (In principle it must *always* be possible to produce a better advertisement than the one you have; but if you keep on seeking to improve it forever, your advertisement will never appear —and advertisements which do not appear do not generate sales!) In an attempt to minimise this problem of comparability, certain companies which have been carrying out advertisement pre-tests for years keep all their past results on computer, and compare each new advertisement with all the historical data. This method unquestionably gives a better indication than any other of whether a new advertisement is really going to be effective, but it can still produce misleading results when a new advertisement has been created which cannot truly be compared with anything done in the past.

Let us now discuss the main methods currently in use for advertisement pre-testing.

1. Testing creative strategy
Obviously ordinary consumers cannot be expected to comprehend and react naturally to the technical jargon used in the definition of a creative strategy. Therefore strategies are converted into written *propositions* which the public can respond to; tests of creative strategies are usually called *Proposition Tests*.

For example, six different strategies for a campaign for a medium priced watch might be expressed in terms of the following *propositions*:

'Consistently the most accurate watch at its price'
'Guaranteed against mechanical defects for 2 years'
'Looks like a watch that costs twice the price'
'The smart watch for the fashion-conscious man'
'Made by craftsmen backed by centuries of horological tradition'
'Used under the roughest conditions by Bloggins' expedition to the Antarctic'

Each proposition reflects a different strategy for advertising watches: accuracy, reliability, expensive appearance, fashionable appearance, traditional expertise, and sturdiness. To choose which is the best a representative sample of prospective watch purchasers would be shown all six on individual cards probably coded 'Watch M, Watch N, Watch Y, Watch Z . . .' (as if they were different watches). The sample would then be asked to choose between the watches, and to give second and third choices. Reasons for their choices would then be probed. Thus the most widely acceptable proposition (or strategy) would be established.

2. (a) Press: concept testing

Concept testing is carried out in basically the same way as proposition testing, except that roughly drawn advertisement concepts are used instead of words on cards. Because the public is not used to looking at rough advertisement concepts, certain precautions need to be taken to avoid the possibility of the research getting side-tracked.

It must be explained in advance to respondents that what they are about to be shown are rough *artist's impressions* of the final advertising. If the final advertising will include photographs, or cartoons, this should be stated.

The drawings in the rough concepts should not be mannered or stylised in any way that might contradict the impression the final advertising is intended to create; they must be as 'bland' as possible. Human beings, especially faces and expressions, are particularly difficult to handle in concept test advertisements; respondents find it very hard not to react to specific but unintended facial characteristics—once again every effort must be made to ensure that the roughly drawn face communicates in *a general way* what is finally intended.

Irrelevant details must be ruthlessly excluded; if the concept artist happens to have drawn cufflinks (unnecessarily) on a shirt, there is a good chance that some respondents will start to worry about why they are there, whether they are fashionable, whether they are gold, and so on.

Headlines should be lettered very clearly, or better still, typeset and stuck into position; ruled lines should be used to indicate where the body copy will be placed, and this must be explained to the respondents.

If all of these precautions have been taken, the concept test should produce sound results. Concept tests are generally used to measure the interest, comprehension and credibility of various different advertising approaches. However, they can also be used to measure impact by means of a *folder test*. In a folder test all the concepts will be spiral-bound together, in the form of a book, and possibly some other 'placebo' advertisements (of no importance) will be interleaved among them. Respondents are given the folder and told to glance through it for say, five minutes. They are then asked what they can remember from the folder, and their memories are probed in detail. Thus folder tests can be used to establish not only what various concepts communicate, but also which of them are most memorable and have greatest impact.

2. (b) Television: storyboard testing

All the provisos listed at the start of the section on press concept testing apply with at least equal force in the case of television storyboard testing: explain first, avoid mannered or stylised drawings, take especial care with human expressions, exclude irrelevant details, and make all sub-titles legible.

Having produced a good storyboard for testing, there are three basic research methods available:

1. The simplest, cheapest, quickest method which usually provides perfectly adequate results is to show the storyboard to respondents, ask them to study it and then obtain their reactions. The public comprehend storyboards (which have been properly prepared for the purpose) far better than might be expected.

2. A rather more sophisticated method is to photograph the storyboard illustrations on to slides and project them while

the interviewer reads the script (or sometimes this is delivered from a synchronised tape recorder).

3. Most sophisticated of all, the storyboard is filmed (or videotaped) with dissolves between the individual frames to simulate movement, and a synchronised tape is produced; to show such a filmed storyboard requires fairly elaborate equipment, of course, and this will influence where and how the research can be undertaken, as we shall see below.

Whichever technique is used, once the respondent has been exposed to the storyboard he (or she) will be asked to recall as much as they can about the commercial, thus testing its memorability. And they will also usually be asked to rate the commercial on a battery of adjectival rating scales of which the most commonly used are:

> *Believable/Unbelievable*
> *Interesting/Uninteresting*
> *Usual/Unusual*
> *Clear/Confusing*
> *Informative/Uninformative*
> *Amusing/Unamusing*
> *Memorable/Unmemorable*
> *Convincing/Unconvincing*
> *Enjoyable/Boring*
> *Would like to see again/Would not like to see again*

Here the value of historic data (sometimes called *normative* data) can easily be seen. It may not be much help to discover, for example, that 47% of respondents think your commercial *Believable* whereas 61% find it *Interesting* and 69% think it *Clear*—unless you know the scores achieved by similar commercials in the past. With the aid of such data it will be possible to analyse the strengths and weaknesses of the new commercial that has been tested—and either make improvements or discard it and start all over again.

Such evidence as exists on the subject (and it is not yet conclusive) suggests that research on storyboards, in whatever form they are tested, produces very much the same results as research on finished filmed commercials; supporting the fact stated above that the public are well able to comprehend and react to storyboard tests so long as these are carried out in the right way.

3.(a) Press: final copy/artwork/proof testing

For both press and television the techniques for testing the finally produced advertisements vary little in fundamental respects from those used in the earlier stages.

The main difference is that by the time the advertisement has reached final production stage there is unlikely to be a wide variety to choose from: advertisers rarely expend the large sums necessary to produce commercials or photographs if they are not confident, as a result of the earlier testing stages, that they are on the right lines. Indeed one of the precise purposes of the earlier research is to avoid the high and wasteful costs involved in producing finished advertisements and commercials which prove to be unusable.

So the purpose of testing the finished article is normally to check that it has in fact achieved the results intended, results which the prior research indicated would be achieved. This is particularly true of press advertisement tests, where pre-testing is almost always carried out at concept stage; it is less true of television commercial tests, because many advertisers do not believe in the reliability of storyboard tests and therefore do not use them (despite the evidence adduced above).

In addition to the folder tests, described above, the two principle methods of testing finished press advertisements are as follows:

1. To paste them into real, printed publications and then carry out research exactly akin to that used in folder tests.
2. To project them as slides, for measured time durations, and obtain recall and reaction data. (This is unlike a tachistoscope test, in that the time duration does not vary. It is always the same for all advertisements tested in this way,

so that different advertisements can be fairly compared via the accumulation of 'normative' data.)

3. (b) Television: final commercial testing

While advertisers may occasionally develop two or three different press advertisements up to the final stage before testing to choose between them, it is rare indeed for two or three different commercials to be produced for testing: the cost would be far too great. Almost invariably then, advertisers find themselves testing single commercials to check whether they have fulfilled their earlier promise, and whether minor alterations (e.g. lengthening the pack shot or adding sub-titling) might improve them still further.

Testing single commercials calls especially for the use of normative historical data to make the results interpretable, and therefore a small group of research companies have specialised in this area and built up considerable data files.

Three of the leading companies in this area, who have also developed unique commercial testing techniques of their own, are:

1. Audience Studies Limited, who operate both in Britain and the United States, and whose speciality (in addition to recall and adjectival rating tests)is an 'interest dial' which respondents turn while watching the commercial to indicate their interest (or lack of interest) as the film proceeds.

2. E. J. Clucas & Associates Limited, whose speciality is to break each commercial down into its component time segments and then to 'force' respondents to analyse their reactions scene by scene.

3. Alpha (U.K.) Research Limited, who use a Quiz Chair which functions in a not dissimilar way to Audience Studies' 'interest dial' except that the respondents press buttons to record positive and negative elements in the commercial.

If these techniques seem almost as if they were drawn from science fiction, and sound a little frightening, then to put the matter in perspective I should perhaps add a comment by

Mark Lovell and Jack Potter whose book on advertising testing is much the best one in the field (see Bibliography): 'All the techniques have their limitations—not least being the dexterity and reaction times of the informants!'

Measuring selling power

As has been said above, no technique yet exists for pre-testing the selling power of an advertisement. However, various attempts have been made to solve this problem and most of them, with the aid of 'normative' data, are useful for particular purposes:

(*a*) *Interest in buying:* respondents are asked 'How would you say the commercial you have just seen tended to increase or decrease your interest in buying the product?' *

	%
Interest increased a lot	14
Interest increased a little	12
Neither increased nor decreased	35
Interest decreased a little	35
Interest decreased a lot	4

Other data in the research showed exactly why those 39% whose interest had decreased had been put off by the commercial.

(*b*) *Pre- and post-intention to buy:* here respondents are given a list of products, including the one being tested, and asked both before and after seeing the commercial their attitudes to buying each of them on the following scale:

Would definitely buy;
Would probably buy;
Might buy;
Probably would not buy;
Definitely would not buy.

* This example is based on an actual case, from the test of a commercial for a dessert.

The shift in response before and after viewing the commercial indicates its sales persuasiveness (or lack of it).

(*c*) *Gift choice:* respondents are told that there is to be a prize draw and asked to select from a list (of products or brands) which of them they would like as a prize, should they win the draw. The product being tested is one of those on the list. After the test commercial has been shown (usually in this instance in company with other commercials and a brief documentary) respondents are informed that their original responses have been mislaid; could they therefore select their desired product once again as the draw is about to take place?

This pre- and post-gift choice system was pioneered in the U.S.A. by Horace Schwerin, one of the key researchers in the field of advertisement testing. It is still widely used, particularly in the United States. However, it is vital to emphasise, as always, that the results it produces must be interpreted with care since certain types of product seem to be particularly susceptible to 'choice swings', while others are almost completely impervious to the system.

How and where can pre-testing techniques be carried out?

We have studied and assessed all the main methods of pre-testing advertisements. But we have not yet considered the question of how and where these techniques can be applied. Many of them can only be effected in particular locations. Here, then, is a list of the ways in which, and the places where, advertising tests can be carried out.

1. In-home structured interviews—These are ideal for proposition tests, concept tests, folder tests, storyboard tests, and pasted-in press advertisement tests. 'Structured' means that the questionnaire is carefully defined and specified in advance.

2. In-home motivational (or depth) interviews—These are used for the same types of test as in structured interviews but instead of the questionnaire being precisely defined in advance, the interviewer will be briefed to encourage respondents' minds and thoughts to wander freely, thus obtaining deeper (but usually mathematically less quantifiable) reactions to the advertisements.

3. Group discussions—These are ideal (and inexpensive) for concept tests, slide or videotaped storyboard tests. Seven or eight respondents from the target market are grouped together in the interviewer's home or in a hotel room where they are prompted and spurred on by the interviewer and by each other and discuss the advertising stimulae they are shown. The discussion is tape-recorded and analysed by an experienced researcher. This is probably the most commonly used method of advertisement testing.

4. Hall tests—These are ideal for tachistoscope tests, slide or videotaped storyboard tests, or videotaped final commercial tests. Respondents are invited into a local church or similar hall where they are exposed, usually one at a time, to the advertisements being tested. Interviewers then administer structural questionnaires. This is obviously a highly artificial situation, but is comparatively inexpensive if a large number of respondents are required at low cost.

5. Theatre tests—These are used particularly for the testing of final commercials (both television and cinema) and sometimes for final press advertisements. Respondents are invited to a cinema or other comfortable hall with projection equipment and suitable seating. Once there they are shown several commercials, sometimes slides of advertisements and a standard 'placebo' documentary. Self-completion questionnaires and special techniques (like the ASL 'interest dial' or the Schwerin gift choice question) can be applied. Theatre tests are extremely expensive, and research companies share out the cost by testing several commercials for different advertisers at once, which in turn makes the system somewhat less flexible than the others described above.

The advertising has now been produced, tested and proved likely to be effective. How can we further measure its real achievements in the very different conditions of the market place?

Testing during and after launch

Once the advertising has started to appear a simple grid can be drawn up to show how its effectiveness can be analysed:

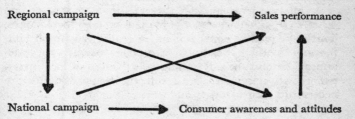

Regional campaign ⟶ Sales performance

National campaign ⟶ Consumer awareness and attitudes

The arrows indicate lines of direct influence. For example, a regional or local campaign will directly influence sales performances in its area and will directly influence consumers' attitudes and awareness (which in turn will directly influence sales performance); and if a regional campaign proves successful it will then be run nationally. Thus in a test situation the various items in the grid interact, and this must be borne in mind as we examine each of them individually.

Regional campaigns

The most reliable method of testing the effectiveness of any advertising is initially to run it in one or two areas of the country only. Today, almost all media groups provide the potential for area testing, and many media positively encourage such tests by providing certain research facilities either free or at a subsidised low cost. Let us consider the area test potential offered by each of the media:

National press: Certain national newspapers—currently

including the *Sun*, *Daily Mirror* and *Daily Mail*—offer advertisers the opportunity to buy space in particular regions of the country, and thus to test new campaigns in those regions. Due to the production costs involved, the newspapers charge a considerable premium for this service; and the areas available tend to be quite large—none smaller than the Tyne Tees TV area (about 6 % of the population). None the less this is an extremely useful service to advertisers on the part of the media concerned.

An alternative means of testing a national press campaign is first to try it in one or more towns, using their local papers. This is frequently done, though in reality it is totally impossible mathematically to correlate exactly (or even approximately) the advertising effectiveness of local newspapers with nationals. As a result, the results obtained are necessarily rather rough and ready; but again, often far better than nothing.

Magazines: IPC Magazines Limited, the leading publishers of weekly and monthly magazines in Britain, offer a unique and exceptionally useful service whereby advertisements can be '*tipped-in*' (i.e. pasted in by hand) to all the copies of their three major women's weeklies sold in any one week, in any one of about 30 towns. Thus it is possible to run a campaign in the 3 magazines involved (*Woman*, *Woman's Own* and *Woman's Weekly*) in, for example, Southampton or Norwich, for a six month or year's test prior to going national. Once again, and perfectly reasonably, IPC Magazines require the advertiser to meet the extra production costs incurred by such tests; and only whole page advertisements (colour or black and white) can be tested.

In addition to this service, it is possible to buy space regionally in the *Readers' Digest*, *Radio Times* and *TV Times*, so that an advertiser wishing to carry out a local test of a magazine campaign is well catered for.

Television: Television is, as we have seen, intrinsically a local as well as a national medium and is thus ideally suited to regional testing. Most of the smaller ITV stations offer special discounts—varying by region and by time of year—for test campaigns; and many additionally offer low-cost research facilities for tests.

The ITV stations most commonly used for tests include *Southern*, *Tyne Tees*, *Anglia* and *Harlech*.

Radio, Cinema and Posters: Like television, each of these media can be used locally or nationally, and therefore can very simply be tested on a regional basis prior to being used nationally. It is important to remember though that radio is still not truly a *national* medium, and its audience is patchy from station to station: grossing up the results achieved on any single station may cause problems. Also remember that the production costs for small cinema and poster test campaigns will unquestionably be disproportionately high.

Below-the-line promotions: Almost all below-the-line promotions can be area-tested prior to national launch. However, in practice such tests are rarely carried out, largely because the costs of below-the-line promotions are not normally sufficiently great to make such testing worth while; and good promotions frequently feature the bulk buying of low-cost premiums, which for small area tests would be most uneconomic.

Direct mail: This is the most easily tested of all the media. Tests do not need to be done on a regional basis: for example, the first 1,000 names can simply be taken from a mailing list of 100,000 and the results achieved can be measured before incurring the cost of the remaining 99,000 mailings. However practical economic difficulties, as with below-the-line promotions, sometimes interfere with such theoretically simple testing operations; and as a result direct mail shots are perhaps less frequently tested than they should be.

Evaluating regional campaigns

The two methods of evaluating regional (and also national) campaigns, as the grid shows, are according to sales performance and according to changes in consumer awareness and attitudes.

Sales performance

It has been made clear throughout the book that (except in the case of direct response coupon advertising) the factors which influence the sales performance of a product or service are many and various; advertising is but one of them, and rarely the most important. However, when a controlled experiment has been carried out in which advertising has been run in one part of the country and not elsewhere, it is generally possible to measure sales results in that area, compare them with the national situation, and impute any differences to the advertising. (However, even here care must be taken. When an experimental campaign is being run company salesmen and even retailers frequently pay undue attention to the product and promote it with a level of effort and enthusiasm that could never be matched on a national basis.)

How are sales measured? The simplest, cheapest, most primitive and least accurate way is via the company's own *ex-factory* sales. Every company nowadays monitors (usually on a computer) its own sales area-by-area; at the very least on a monthly but normally on a weekly or even sometimes on a daily basis. It is normally a comparatively easy administrative matter to isolate the company's sales in the area where the advertising test is running and compare them with sales elsewhere. The serious disadvantage of relying on ex-factory sales as a measure of advertising effectiveness is that, except in the case of companies who sell *direct to the public*, these sales figures can give no indication whatsoever of what is happening to sales in the retail and wholesale trade. Ex-factory sales may increase because retailers have been cajoled into taking more stock (as they usually are in a test situation); or they may decrease because a few retailers have decided to run down their stocks. Neither case will correctly reflect the quantities being bought by customers. Thus ex-factory sales are an unreliable indicator of an advertising campaign's effectiveness, especially in the short term.

Instead most large companies now obtain regular *retail sales audits*, which measure once every two months the actual volume of a product purchased from shops by customers. Retail sales audits work in this way: a market research company recruits a national sample panel of retailers which will be representative of, say, all the grocers, or all the chemists in the country. Such a sample is likely to comprise 800–1,500 shops. Then sales audit executives call upon the sample shops once every two months. On each visit they will first look to see whether Product X is in stock at all. If it is, they will count the stock, find out how many packets of Product X the store has ordered since the last visit two months ago, check back to see what the shop's stock was two months previously, and thus calculate exactly how much Product X has been sold in the period. By adding together the sales in the total sample of shops the market research company is able to total the true *consumer* sales achieved by Product X during the two-month period. (In reality the sales audit executive does not merely check Product X but all of its competitors and a wide range of other products for the many manufacturers who are purchasing sales audit data.)

As well as providing data on consumer sales, by making maximum use of his visit to the retailer the sales audit executive (and thus his market research company) is also able to give the manufacturer of Product X the following information:

Retailers' purchases of Product X (to correlate with ex-factory sales);

Percentage of shops which stock Product X;
Percentage of shops displaying Product X;
Total volume of stocks of Product X in retail shops;
Average price at which Product X is being sold;
Month's supply of Product X in stock;
Sales of Product X's competitors;
(All above data for Product X's competitors);
Product X's market share.

All of this information will be available nationally, regionally and as time goes by, historically; all of which can greatly help a manufacturer seeking to assess the results of his advertising campaign.

The leading company carrying out retail sales audits in the U.K., the U.S.A. and throughout Europe is the *A. C. Nielsen Company*, which is the largest research company in the world. In the U.K. two other companies also offer sales audit research though they are smaller than A. C. Nielsen: *Stats MR Limited*, and *Retail Audits Limited*.

A different approach to the measurement of consumer sales performance is to obtain purchase data on a continuous basis from a sample of consumers. One way of doing this is to get them to fill in detailed diaries of their purchases; another is to get them to throw all the empty packets of products they use into a special bag which is then collected by the research company each week or month. (This is the so-called 'Dustbin' research.) The advantages of these methods over retail sales audits are:

(*i*) They take account of direct-selling companies (like Avon Cosmetics) whose products never go through retailers;
(*ii*) They take account of sales through retailers who do not allow retail audits in their shops (for example, Boots Chemists);
(*iii*) They show not only *how much* is being bought, but *who* is buying, thus giving consumer profile as well as sales data.

The disadvantages of these methods are that a large and

expensive sample is needed to achieve accuracy, particularly for minority usage products; and that for certain products they are unsuitable because members of a family often do not want others in the family to know how much they consume. (It has been shown, for example, that housewives tend to lie about their cigarette consumption if their husbands are with them during an interview.) Nevertheless consumer purchase panels are favoured by many manufacturers and the two leading ones in the U.K. are the *Television Consumer Audit* which mostly covers grocery and household goods; and the *Toiletries, Cosmetics and Perfumery Index*, run by *Audits of Great Britain Limited*.

Consumer awareness and attitudes

The methods for measuring consumers' awareness and attitudes were covered in detail on pages 132–35 and do not require reiterating here. In a regional test, surveys would be carried out both in the test area and nationally so that the effects of the advertising on awareness and attitudes could be immediately seen. This is essential back-up information for retail sales audit data, since it will be important for the advertiser to know whether his campaign is simply persuading old customers to buy more (but not increasing awareness and interest levels among non-customers); or whether his campaign is genuinely reaching out to new customers. (Both would result in an increase in retail sales, but the advertising would be achieving quite different effects in each case.)

National campaign

Assuming that the advertising has successfully undergone all the rigours of pre-testing and regional testing—and that is a large assumption, since it has been estimated that only one in fifteen campaigns clears all the hurdles—the advertiser will be ready to launch it nationally.

Once launched nationally its effectiveness will be doubly

difficult to measure, and Lord Leverhulme's original dictum will once more come into its own. However, the wise advertiser will continue to check regularly his retail sales audits, his consumer purchase data, and his awareness and attitudes information. And finally, he will keep a close watch on his profit and loss account: as long as his profits are increasing it is reasonable to assume that his advertising is achieving at least some success.

Think Exercises

1. 'I never bother with market research,' a successful entrepreneur tells you. 'I simply produce what the public wants at a price I know it will pay.' Try to persuade him that despite his scepticism market research could be of help to him none the less.

2. Think of half-a-dozen noteworthy 'fashion' changes in product and service usage over recent years (e.g. the wearing of denim, the decline in cinema visiting). Why did each of these changes occur? Were they prompted by 'fashion leaders'? By advertising? By technological change? By other forces?

3. 'Market research isn't a science. Look how often the political polls predict the wrong answers!' But accurate prediction is only one aspect of the definition of a science. (Biology and medicine are sciences, though they are not as 'predictive' as physics and chemistry.) Argue the cases for and against the proposition that market research *is* a science despite its fallibility.

7

Controlling Advertising

At one time, before the word *consumerism* had even been
invented, the trading laws of Britain and the United States
were based upon the principles of *caveat emptor*: let the buyer
beware. It was the responsibility of the purchaser (rather
than the seller) to ensure that the goods and services he
obtained for his money were what they purported to be. The
onus was upon the purchaser to consider carefully whether
they were worth the price being asked before he parted with
his hard-earned cash: let the buyer beware.

This inequitable balance of power between buyer and
seller inevitably led to unscrupulous sellers taking advantage
of their strength. In advertising, it led to ruthless merchants
making wholly unachievable and unjustifiable claims for
their products. Look at some of these headlines (all taken
from Leonard de Vries' marvellous book *Victorian Advertisements*; see Bibliography):

DR SCOTT'S ELECTRIC HAIR BRUSH
Warranted to Cure:
Nervous Headache
Bilious Headache in 5 minutes
Neuralgia

The Two Infallible Powers:
THE POPE AND BOVRIL

VASPO CRESOLENE
Cures While You Sleep
Whooping Cough—Croup—Asthma—Colds

HOVIS
Forms Good Bone, Brain, Flesh and Muscle

Needless to say, such nineteenth-century excesses of advertising exuberance could not appear today. Consumers are protected against advertisements that are not 100% legal, decent, honest and truthful both by the law and by the advertising industry itself. The unequal balance of power between buyers and sellers has been redressed. Today the buyers must still beware; but so too must the sellers.

In advertising as in all other areas of human activity, there are only two methods by which possible misdemeanour can be averted. The perpetrators can be stopped either before the misdemeanour has been committed—this is the ideal; or they can be brought to book as soon as possible afterwards—this is often all that is realistically feasible. Generally speaking, the law relies upon the second method; it deals with those who have committed offences. If you wish people to apply the first method you must, again generally speaking, rely upon their own self-discipline. Advertising controls employ both methods: legal and self-disciplinary.

Legal controls

Although for centuries particular laws and regulations had applied to the composition and marking of certain goods, until the latter half of the nineteenth century there was no general body of law on the subject. In 1860, the first Act was passed to cover the composition and sale of Food and Drugs, followed by the Weights and Measures Act in 1878 and the Merchandise Marks Act in 1887. The first two have their modern counterparts in the Acts of 1955 and 1963 of the same names, while the third has become the best known and of most direct concern to advertisers, the Trades Descriptions Act of 1968. This Act for the first time specifically stated in law that the contents of an advertisement could constitute a trade description.

Until nearly the end of the nineteenth century, the prin-

cipal remedy for a customer in respect of goods purchased
was a Common Law action for breach of contract, requiring
proof that the goods were either basically different from
what had been ordered or that there had been a false
inducement to buy them. A typical and famous example is
that of Carhill and the Carbolic Smoke Ball Company. In
1892 a company which manufactured a curious medica-
ment called the Carbolic Smoke Ball inserted the following
advertisement in the *Pall Mall Gazette*:

> '£100 reward will be paid by the Carbolic Smoke
> Ball Company to any person who contracts the increas-
> ing epidemic influenza, colds or any disease caused by
> taking cold, after having used the Ball three times daily
> for two weeks according to the printed directions
> supplied with each Ball. £1,000 is deposited with the
> Alliance Bank, Regent Street, showing our sincerity
> in the matter.'

On the strength of this advertisement a Mrs Carhill bought
the Ball and used it as directed. After more than the required
fortnight of use she contracted influenza and so claimed the
£100 reward. The Company refused to pay. Mrs Carhill
brought a civil action under Common Law claiming the
money as due to her under a contract between the Company
and herself. The Company maintained that no such contract
existed, that the advertisement was a mere 'puff' and was
not intended to create legal obligations. The Court of
Appeal rejected these arguments, held that the advertisement had created a contract and ruled that Mrs Carhill was
entitled to her £100.

Following the case of Carhill and the Carbolic Smoke
Ball Company, in 1893 the Sale of Goods Act was passed,
which increased consumers' civil remedies over and above
those available at Common Law if, for a variety of reasons,
goods were below standard. This was an important Act and
can still be regarded as the backbone of all civil consumer
legislation. None the less civil remedies continued to be

available only under the broad laws of contract if goods proved faulty, until an important case of negligence in 1932.

In that year a young woman bought a stone bottle of ginger beer and gave it to her friend to drink. Her friend found a partially decomposed snail in it and was, not altogether unnaturally, ill. The young woman as purchaser,

and therefore party to the contract with the shopkeeper, did not sue as she had suffered no damage personally. The friend could not sue as she had no contract with the shopkeeper. So she tried the manufacturer not in contract but in negligence, this seeming to be her only possible legal redress. Her chances were slim because until that time the law did not recognise a general duty of care by manufacturers towards their customers. However, the House of Lords decided, on appeal, that such a duty existed. Thus was established, for the first time, a clear definition of a manufacturer's responsibility to the ultimate consumer of his product.

The basic principles having been established, during the past two decades there has been a welter of legislation either directly or indirectly controlling advertisements, and the

British Code of Advertising Practice (of which you will read more below) now lists over sixty statutes and statutory instruments which have special relevance to advertising. Of these unquestionably the most significant is the Trade Descriptions Act, 1968. This Act largely implemented the recommendations of the Molony Committee on Consumer Protection in 1962 which, incidentally, for the first time defined the concept of 'consumer protection' in the following words:

> 'It consists of those instances where the law inter-venes to impose safeguards in favour of purchasers and hire purchasers, together with the activities of a number of organisations, variously inspired, the object or effect of which is to procure fair and satisfying treatment for the domestic buyers. From another viewpoint, consumer protection may be regarded as those measures which contribute directly or indirectly, to the consumer's assurance that he will buy goods of suitable quality appropriate to this purpose: that they will give him reasonable use, and that if he has a just complaint there will be a means of redress.'

Trades Description Act, 1968

The 1968 *Trades Description Act* is particularly noteworthy for its effect in three areas:

1. Advertising in and on retail premises became subject to legal control for the first time.
2. Members of the public wishing to complain were invited to do so through their local Inspector of Weights and Measures, who could then institute legal proceedings if his investigations showed there to be a case to answer. (The Merchandise Marks Act, 1963 had been ineffective largely because individuals with complaints had to institute actions personally and most people were unwilling to go to such trouble and risk possible costs.)

3. 'Bargain' and 'sale' prices came under strict control; if in any form of advertisement goods are offered at a reduced price then the Act requires that the same goods must have been offered for sale by the advertiser at a higher price for a continuous period of at least 28 days during the preceding 6 months.

Under the Act the following qualify as 'trade descriptions' and are therefore subject to the law, so that any *false* description is prosecutable:

    (a) Quantity, size or gauge;

    (b) Method of manufacture, production, processing or reconditioning;

    (c) Composition;

    (d) Fitness for purpose, strength, performance, behaviour or accuracy.

    (e) Any physical characteristics not included in the preceding paragraphs;

    (f) Testing by any person and the results thereof;

    (g) Conforming with a type approved by any person;

    (h) Place or date of manufacture, production, processing or reconditioning;

    (i) Person by whom manufactured, produced, processed or reconditioned;

    (j) Other history, including previous ownership or use.

Moreover *anybody* responsible for a false trade description, including the manufacturer, the advertising agency, and even the individual copywriter may be indictable under the Act. Great care must therefore now be employed to ensure that all factual descriptions in advertisements are wholly and absolutely accurate.

Other important legislation

Apart from the Trades Descriptions Act 1968, the twenty most significant among the sixty or so statutes affecting advertising are the following:

Advertisements (Hire Purchase) Act, 1967—Regulates advertisements giving hire purchase terms.

Betting, Gaming and Lotteries Act, 1963—Declares lotteries illegal, controls prize competitions and controls advertising of betting shops.

Companies Act, 1948—Regulates prospectuses inviting the public to invest money in companies.

Copyright Act, 1956—Concerns copyright in all matters, including advertising material in all media.

Consumer Protection Act, 1961 (amended 1971)—Concerns regulations requiring packets etc. to carry safety warnings and instructions for use.

Criminal Justice Act, 1972—Provides that those convicted of offences against, for example, the Trades Description Act may be ordered to pay compensation.

Fair Trading Act, 1973—Provides for the appointment of a Director-General of Fair Trading and staff to keep a close and continuous watch upon consumers' interests.

Food and Drugs Act, 1955 (and subsequent amendments)—Details requirements as to advertising and labelling of foods.

Indecent Advertisement Act, 1889—Provides penalties for indecent advertisements.

Independent Broadcasting Authority Act, 1973—Controls advertising on both commercial television and radio.

Medicines Act, 1968—Regulates advertisements for medicines, which must conform to the terms of a licence issued by the Medicines Commission.

Patents (International Conventions) Act, 1938—Defines application of trademarks as trade descriptions.

Prevention of Fraud (Investments) Act, 1958 (as amended)—Governs statements made in advertisements inducing persons to invest.

Race Relations Act, 1968—Prohibits advertisements discriminating on grounds of race, colour, ethnic or national origin.

Sale of Goods Act, 1893—Still especially important with

regard to items and conditions stated or implied in mail order advertisements.

Town and Country Planning Act, 1962—Controls outdoor advertising.

Trades Description Act, 1972—Requires indication of origin of certain imported goods.

Trading Stamps Act, 1964—Lays down conditions for trading stamp operations.

Unsolicited Goods and Services Act, 1971—Determines the rights and duties of recipients of unsolicited goods.

Weights and Measures Act, 1963 (and regulations thereunder) —Lays down requirements for weights and measures on labels and packs.

Thus it will be seen that advertising is rigorously controlled in the U.K.

Independent Broadcasting Authority Act, 1973

Before we come to the additional voluntary controls which the advertising industry imposes upon itself, we must consider the strict regulations within which commercial television and radio function in the U.K. The 1973 Act set up an Independent Broadcasting Authority (similar to the Independent Television Authority, set up for TV only by the original 1955 Independent Television Act) which has the following statutory duties:

(*a*) To exclude from broadcasting any advertisement which would be likely to mislead;

(*b*) To draw up and from time to time review a Code governing standards and practice in advertising, and prescribing the advertisements and methods of advertising to be prohibited or prohibited in particular circumstances; and

(*c*) to secure compliance with the Code.

Pursuant to its duties, the IBA publishes a *Code of Advertising*

Practice which specifies its attitudes to advertising generally and includes three detailed appendices concerning:

1. Advertising and children
2. Finance advertising
3. Advertising of medicines and treatments

The Code is drawn up by the IBA in consultation with its Advertising Advisory Committee, a Medical Advisory Panel and the Home Secretary. The Code is then published and applied in the following way:

1. Advertisers and agencies submit scripts to the IBA's Advertising Control Department (approximately 7,000 draft TV scripts are submitted for approval each year).
2. IBA and Programme Companies check facts, assess evidence, assess method of presentation. Where necessary, advice of specialist consultants is obtained.
3. Discussions with advertiser/agency. Agreement, amendment or rejection follows (1,700 scripts a year need amendment).
4. Commercial filmed or recorded on videotape.
5. IBA and Programme Companies view finished commercial.
6. Agreement, amendment or rejection (about 200 filmed commercials returned for amendment each year).

This process can be time-consuming, though the IBA co-operates in every way possible to make it as speedy as it can, and there are sometimes vexed discussions between advertisers, their agencies and the Authority when the various parties do not interpret the Code in precisely the same way.

However, everyone concurs that the IBA's careful and sensible pre-vetting of all broadcast commercials (sound radio commercials must comply with the same Code) results in the exceptionally high standards achieved by British commercials in accordance with the Code's own opening statement:

'The general principle governing all broadcast advertising is that it should be legal, decent, honest and truthful. It is recognised that this principle is not peculiar to broadcasting but is one which applies to all reputable advertising in other media in this country. Nevertheless, broadcasting, and particularly television, because of its greater intimacy within the home, gives rise to problems which do not necessarily occur in other media and it is essential to maintain a consistently high quality of broadcast advertising.'

Voluntary controls

Because of the comparatively small number of new television commercials produced—none the less amounting to over 100 per week—the task of pre-vetting and approving *before* transmission is a manageable one. To do the same in all press media would be virtually impossible. In a recent year 905,000 display advertisements by national advertisers were monitored in national and provincial newspapers and magazines alone. This figure excludes all small local newspapers, trade and technical publications, local advertisers and all classified advertisements. Even continuing to exclude the classifieds, an estimate of 2,000,000 new advertisements in all press media each year cannot be too far wide of the mark: to pre-vet them would involve setting up an organisation able to check all the facts and details in 40,000 new advertisements every week. On the basis of the IBA's staff-to-advertisement ratio, this would involve a small governmental department with a staff of about 15,000!

This is obviously not feasible. Instead, the advertising industry has undertaken to keep its own house in order through a system of self-imposed controls which, of necessity, can only be applied to advertisements after they have been published and are seen to be wrong, usually by a member of the public. (In addition, the advertisement departments of all newspapers and magazines keep a wary eye open for advertisements which should not be allowed to appear, and frequently hold them up at least until they have been convinced that the advertisements are in fact acceptable.)

How it works

The advertising voluntary control system in the U.K. is operated under the jurisdiction of the Advertising Standards Authority (ASA), an independent body set up and paid for by the advertising industry to ensure that its system of self-regulation works in the public interest. The Authority has an independent chairman, and its members are appointed by him to serve as individuals and not as representatives of any sectional interest. Half of the members must be from outside advertising. The Authority maintains close contact with central and local government departments, and with consumer organisations and trade associations.

Like the IBA, the ASA controls advertising through the publication of a regulatory Code, known as the British Code of Advertising Practice. The first such Code was published in 1962, since when it has been regularly revised and updated, and has gone through five editions; it now runs to over 60 pages of densely packed type. The Code is drawn up by organisations representing advertisers, advertising agencies and media. It is administered by a committee called the Code of Advertising Practice (CAP) Committee whose members, all experienced in advertising, are drawn from the following organisations all of which subscribe to the contents of the Code:

> Advertising Association
> Association of Independent Radio Contractors
> Association of Mail Order Publishers
> British Mail Advertising Association
> British Poster Advertising Association
> Bus Advertising Council
> Direct Mail Producers Association

Electrical Sign Manufacturers Association
Incorporated Society of British Advertisers
Independent Television Companies Association
Institute of Practitioners in Advertising
Master Sign Makers Association
Newspaper Publishers Association
Newspaper Society
Periodical Publishers Association
Proprietary Association of Great Britain
Scottish Daily Newspaper Society
Scottish Newspaper Proprietors Association
Screen Advertising Association
Solus Outdoor Advertising Association

The sanctions, which give the essential bite to the Code, are primarily applied by those media which are party to its provisions. The media will neither publish nor accept any advertisement which infringes the Code, nor any advertisement currently under investigation by the ASA and/or the CAP Committee. To these commercial sanctions (no advertiser wishes to have his advertising *banned* by the media) have recently been added the sanction of adverse publicity. This is wielded by the ASA which regularly publishes details of its investigations and names those who have offended against the Code. Again, reputable advertisers try hard to avoid unsavoury publicity of this kind.

Since the system is based, to a considerable extent, upon complaints being raised by members of the public against advertisements they believe to have broken the Code, the ASA runs advertising with the objective of encouraging public complaints. This campaign began in April 1975. Until then complaints had been running at the rate of approximately twenty-five per week. Predictably the campaign initially generated a great upsurge in the number of complaints, and 1,000 were received by the ASA in the first eight weeks. However, the number has now fallen back to an average only a little above its original running rate—

evidence of the success of the Code's enforcement throughout the advertising industry.

The finance necessary to fund the ASA, the CAP Committee, a secretariat of about thirty people, and the advertising campaign, amounts to £300,000–£400,000 per year. This is raised by a levy of 0·1 % on the cost of all advertising in the press, magazines, on posters, by direct mail, and in the cinema. (The remit of the ASA does not extend to the two broadcast media which, as we have seen, are the responsibility of the IBA.)

The levy is raised by agencies from advertisers and paid to a body controlling the finances of the complete operation, called the Advertising Standards Board of Finance Limited.

The British Code of Advertising Practice, like the IBA Code, starts with general principles which apply to all advertising and then follows with regulations which apply to the following specific categories:

Alcohol	Commemor-	Mail order
Artificial	ative items	Property
sweeteners	Employment	Retail sales
Betting	Financial	Sales promotions
Tipsters	Franchise	Self-defence
Charitable	schemes	courses
causes	Homework	TV and other
Cigarettes and	schemes	appliances on
Tobacco	Inclusive tours	rental

Separate sections and appendices of the Code then follow, which relate to:

Medicinal products
The Identification of
    Advertisements (as advertisements)
Children and Young People
Slimming Products
Consumer Credit
Consumer Investments

Mail Order
Diseases to which no reference may be made
Hair and Scalp Products

Clearly it is not possible to reprint here the complete 60-page Code (though you should certainly obtain a copy for yourself from the Advertising Standards Authority, 15–17 Ridgmount Street, London, WC1E 7AW), but it is worth once again quoting its preamble, as this sets and defines the tone of all British advertising:

'All advertisements should be legal, decent, honest and truthful.'
'All advertisements should be prepared with a sense of responsibility to the consumer.'
'All advertisements should conform to the principles of fair competition as generally accepted in business.'

'No advertisement should bring advertising into disrepute or reduce confidence in advertising as a service to industry and to the public.'

Problem Areas

Mention has already been made, both in the section covering the IBA code and in the section on the CAP above, of certain particular problem advertising areas: cigarettes and tobacco goods, alcohol, medicines and advertising to children—each of which it is worth briefly touching upon in more detail.

Cigarettes and Tobacco Goods

The advertising of cigarettes is not now permitted on television, nor in the cinema with films produced for young audiences; cigars and pipe tobacco advertisements are, however, still allowed in all media.

Cigarette advertisements in the media in which they are accepted are subject to a special section of the CAP, Appendix M, which has been drawn up and agreed between the cigarette manufacturers and the government. The essence of the Cigarette Advertising Code (as stated) is as follows:

'Advertisements should not seek to encourage people, particularly the young, to start smoking, or if they are already smokers, to increase their level of smoking or to smoke to excess; and should not exploit those who are especially vulnerable, in particular young people or those who suffer from any physical, mental or social handicap.'

Alcohol

The IBA operates no ban, but manufacturers of spirits and liqueurs by voluntary agreement do not advertise on commercial television. Both the IBA Code and the CAP Com-

mittee however do specify that liquor advertising must not
be addressed to the young, and that no one drinking in an
advertisement should seem to be younger than 25. No alcohol advertisement may feature or foster immoderate drinking, nor in any way link drinking with driving.

Medicines

The wide variety of medicines available has inevitably
meant that the regulations in both the IBA Code and the
CAP are copious and exacting. Moreover, there is every
likelihood that the government may tighten the rules still
further in future legislation, as it is highly concerned about
the possible abuses of medicines. Currently, the basic principles of the two Codes with regard to medicine advertising
are that all such advertising must be for products licensed
under the Medicines Act, 1968, and must comply with the
provisions of the product's licence.

Perhaps the most important other proviso, in both codes,
is that no advertisement may claim or imply the *cure* of any
ailment, illness or disease, as distinct from the relief of the
symptoms.

Children

Here the regulations are frequently of an ethical, yet
common sense kind, aimed at protecting children from
hazards and dangers. In addition, the IBA Code lists products which may not be advertised either in children's programmes or before 9.00 p.m. Above all, the Codes require
advertisers to keep in mind the following fundamental
approach in the matter of children and advertising:

> 'No product or service may be advertised and no
> method of advertising may be used ... which large
> numbers of children are likely to see or hear which
> might result in harm to them physically, mentally or
> morally, and no method of advertising may be em-

ployed which takes advantage of the natural credulity and sense of loyalty of children.'

We have now seen how both the law and voluntary controls combine to protect the consumer, so that advertisers can no longer make such wildly exaggerated claims as we saw at the beginning of this chapter—amusing though they may be to us today.

The international situation

So far, we have primarily been considering the control of advertising in the U.K. However, advertising control systems now exist in at least thirty countries, including the U.S.A., Canada and all of the EEC members. These controls are applied in three ways:

1. National legislation;
2. The International Code of Advertising Practice;
3. Local self-regulatory Codes and regulations.

There is not time here to cover the many legislative Acts which most of the world's countries have enacted over the

years to protect the consumer from unscrupulous or misleading advertising. Suffice it to say that the simple principle of *caveat emptor* no longer applies anywhere in the
world. In the EEC countries and in the United States in
particular there is a heavy (and growing) volume of legislation controlling the content of advertisements. (In Washington alone, more than twenty different federal administrative
bodies exercise controls over advertising.)

The International Code of Advertising Practice—first issued in
1937 and later revised in 1949, 1955, 1966 and 1973—is a
self-regulatory Code sponsored by the International Cham-
ber of Commerce, based in France. This Code, to which the
individual advertising industries of the world's leading
countries adhere, is of necessity fairly broad in its approach.
Applying to so many countries, it does not seek to regulate in
detail the advertising of each of them individually. Nevertheless its stated first principle is identical to that of the
British Code of Advertising Practice:

> 'All advertising should be legal, decent, honest and
> truthful.'

Again, we have not the time here to cover the individual
self-regulatory systems of every country. The majority are
based upon the same working structure, and the same principles, as the system in the U.K.: an independent authority,
comprised of people both from within advertising and
without, backed-up by a small secretariat charged with
ensuring that the self-regulatory system functions efficiently.

In the United States the situation is especially complex,
because there is both federal and state legislation affecting
advertising, and federal and state self-regulatory bodies.
The question has also arisen as to whether a national,
industry-wide regulatory effort would represent a violation
of the anti-trust doctrines supported by Congressional
statutes.

However, a single, centralised body now exists to supervise all *national* advertising. This is:

National Advertising Review Board (NARB)
850 Third Avenue,
New York City 10022.

NARB is sponsored by the four leading trade associations concerned with advertising in the U.S.A.—the American Advertising Federation, the American Association of Advertising Agencies, the Association of National Advertisers, and the Council of Better Business Bureaux. Like the British Advertising Standards Authority, it is completely autonomous, and controls the content of advertisements by the twin sanctions of bad publicity (NARB also publishes reports on offending advertisements) and media rejection of advertisements deemed unacceptable.

Before leaving the subject of advertising controls it is worth looking at a subject that has become something of a battle-ground in recent years, where antagonists on both sides have all too often taken up extremist stances. This is the subject of consumerism.

'Consumerism'

The concept of *consumerism* (though not the word) probably originated in a book published in the United States in 1927 entitled *Your Money's Worth*. In *Your Money's Worth* the two young authors, Chase and Schlink, reported the results of tests made on products for the American government by the National Bureau of Standards. The tests showed that quality as measured by the Bureau frequently failed to find a sensible reflection in prices, and that many poor-quality goods cost more than higher-quality goods and vice versa. The book became an immediate best-seller. Schlink then teamed up with another writer, Arthur Kallet, to write *One Hundred Million Guinea Pigs* which turned the spotlight on advertisers as well as on the products themselves. The American Consumers' Union grew out of the interest generated by these books.

In Britain the consumerist movement did not really begin

until thirty years later when in 1957 a small group of enthusiasts produced the first copy of *Which?*, the consumer magazine. They printed 10,000 copies which were quickly sold, and since then the circulation of *Which?*, together with membership of its parent, the Consumers' Association, has grown to approximately 600,000. In Europe, Scandinavia particularly, consumerism has become a powerful force backed to an ever-increasing extent by governments and legislation.

What precisely is *consumerism*? The word is a neologism, derived of course from *consumer*, which is appositely defined by the Shorter Oxford Dictionary as 'He who or that which consumes ... as opposed to produces', the emphasis of recent years being on the word *opposed*. The theory of consumerism is simple enough: today's mammoth companies are extremely powerful in their own interests, and the individual customer alone is virtually powerless against them. Thus to exert an influence individual customers (consumers) must join together, in much the same way that the nineteenth-century labourers joined together into trades unions. Even the largest companies cannot ignore the combined pressure of 600,000 shoppers in concert. Moreover, in addition to exerting pressures with their purses, by not buying goods which they believe to be badly made or poor value, consumerists have sought to obtain—and have achieved—adverse publicity for those companies whom they consider to be deliberately producing inadequate products. Probably the most famous case of this kind was American consumerist Ralph Nader's battle with General Motors over the safety (or rather lack of safety) of several of their models.

Nobody likes to be criticised, perhaps least of all such large and powerful institutions as major industrial companies, whose executives fundamentally believe that they are devoting their lives to producing to the best of their ability products which the public wants; and wants sufficiently to be prepared to pay good money for. Businessmen, therefore, tended to react angrily, unnecessarily angrily, to the consumerists' criticisms. General Motors' instigation of a secret enquiry into Ralph Nader's private life was a particular example of such an over-reaction.

All intelligent consumerists recognise that the public needs and relies upon a wide choice of goods and services, and that these goods and services are generally best produced by competing private enterprises, which need to make reasonable profits in order to finance their own future growth. Indeed, without competitive private enterprise consumerism would soon be dead. There would be no need for all those complex charts in consumer magazines comparing the qualities and deficiencies of innumerable makes if the State produced the single model it believed to be the best—as that would be the only one available.

Consumerists have noisily pointed out certain things that they have found to be wrong with products that are on sale. Sometimes they have been right, sometimes they have been wrong. But wise marketing and advertising people should always keep an alert ear cocked in their direction. The views consumerists express today will often (though by no means always) be views which the public will espouse tomorrow; and to ignore them would be perilous.

Think Exercises

1 'The self-regulatory control of advertising is a phoney whitewash,' somebody says to you at a party, 'devised by advertisers to stop the Government bringing in legislation they are afraid of.' Try to convince him of the advantages of self-regulation over legal controls.

2. Search through half a dozen newspapers looking for advertisements which you suspect may infringe the Code of Advertising Practice. Study carefully any which seem to sail particularly close to the wind. Think whether they could be made less questionable without reducing their

effectiveness. (And if you *do* find any that you think break the Code, write to the ASA!)

3. Despite their length and comprehensive coverage, some critics of advertising complain that the IBA Code and the Code of Advertising Practice are not nearly rigorous enough. While searching through the newspapers for question 2, and while looking at commercials, see if there are any areas of advertising where it seems to you that the Code ought to be strengthened. Good taste? Patent medicine claims? Safety? Then think also of the possible difficulties and disadvantages that might arise from such 'strengthening' of the Codes.

8

The International Scene

Approximately 2,000 major companies today operate on a worldwide scale. Comparatively few of them, perhaps regrettably, are British. More than half are American; the majority of the rest are Japanese or from other European countries. Britain's membership of the EEC has so far given but a modest boost to most companies' international aspirations. Nevertheless, every British businessman knows that even if the trend towards international trading has taken place more slowly than was predicted a decade ago, the trend is none the less inexorable.

With each year that passes the world grows smaller, in that the time taken to get from one place to another decreases. At the same time, paradoxically, the countries and markets of the world are becoming less homogeneous. As air travel and rapid international communications continuously shrink the globe, chauvinism and national individuality grow stronger. How does this inconsistent pattern affect advertising?

International advertising reflects the basic problems inherent in international trading. These can be summed up as follows:

1. To what extent are human needs and requirements uniform throughout the world?
2. To what extent are peoples and markets so disparate that each country, each region and even each locality demands its own particular approach?

Everybody knows that in certain respects the French are

totally different from the British—they eat snails and frogs legs, cook better, bathe less and drink about twenty times as much wine per head of population annually. Yet in other respects they are amazingly similar—they live in a mixed socialist/capitalist democracy, smoke heavily, wear much

the same kinds of clothes and drink quantities of Coca-Cola. An identical to-and-fro picture will be found to exist for any two countries you choose to compare. For the businessman and especially for the advertiser, the problem is to identify correctly the areas of similarity and dissimilarity. How can this be done?

Analysing markets internationally

It is first necessary to differentiate between multi-national companies, which have manufacturing and marketing subsidiaries in most of the larger countries, and national companies which export their products (usually via sales agents working on commission) to all corners of the globe. Multi-national companies will have organisations on the ground in the relevant markets, who will be able to provide a knowledgeable assessment of the local situation. National companies will usually need to make their own assessment from headquarters, with little or no local help.

For national companies the first task will be to obtain hard and reliable background data. This is less difficult than it sounds. The U.K. sources of data mentioned on pages 142–5 all have considerable information about other countries, particularly in Europe. Additional sources from which information can be obtained are:

> Trade Associations (e.g. Brewers' Society, British Radio Equipment Manufacturers' Association, International Tea Council)
> Embassies and Trade Centres
> Bulletins issued by Banks (e.g. Lloyds Bank Review)
> Trade Magazines
> International Publications (particularly Readers' Digest, Time, Newsweek, Vision)
> U.K. Central Statistical Office
> UNESCO and FAO Yearbooks
> UN Yearbook of National Accounts Statistics
> Institute of Practitioners in Advertising—International Advertising Leaflets

Many of these sources will inevitably lead you on to others so that with diligence and time, it will be possible to unearth substantial information about almost any market, in almost any country in the world. The key facts that must be initially established are:

> Overall trends—is the market expanding/static/declining?
> Competitive situation—which local/multinational companies are involved?
> Maker's/brand shares—which manufacturers have substantial market shares?
> Distribution/retailing patterns
> Price structures

Ownership of relevant goods (e.g. cars *re* petrol, pets *re* petfoods)

Broad population and socio-economic trends

Advertising expenditures

Attitudinal and motivational research (if available)

With the accumulation of such data it will become possible to make a realistic assessment of the problems and opportunities for your particular product or company. Most important, a picture will begin to emerge of the ways in which each market under consideration seems to be like, or unlike, the U.K. market and any others with which you may be familiar.

As the picture builds up you are likely to be surprised by the diversity rather than by the homogeneity of markets and products throughout the world. Here are just some of the major consumer product fields where tastes, brands and habits vary widely from country to country:

Automobiles	Cigarettes	Holidays
Beer	Confectionary	Publishing
Bread	Electrical appliances	Retailing

And here, on the other hand, are some of the product fields where the same brands and makes reappear whichever country you consider:

Airline travel	Carbonated drinks	Margarines
Breakfast cereals		Petrol
Car hire	Cosmetics Hair products	Watches and clocks

In not one of these fields, let it be re-emphasised, will the market situation be exactly the same, or completely different, from one country to another. Even within the small area of Britain, wide local disparities exist in the consumption of different products. Handrolling cigarettes, for example, is almost totally a Southern practice; whereas in the North East young girls consume Snowballs (advokaat and lemonade) in far greater quantities than they do anywhere else in the country!

International advertising

International advertising predictably reflects these marketing complexities. As with national advertising, international advertising problems may be broken down into two broad areas, 'Media' and 'Creative', which will now be considered separately.

Media problems

Once the background marketing data detailed above has been assembled, it will be necessary to define the *target market* for the campaign, in precisely the same way as would have been done in the U.K. It may not be possible to draw the identikit picture with quite such precision in some countries, particularly smaller ones, where less research information is available. None the less, before any campaign is planned, anywhere in the world, it is *essential* always to make at least a rough attempt at defining the target market. Indeed in some respects it is even more vital to carry out this task in foreign countries than it is at home, since you will have less intuitive 'feel' for the situation. We would all know instinctively that the *Financial Times* is an unlikely medium with which to try and reach housewives cost-effectively—but what about *Le Monde* or *Der Spiegel* or *The Washington Post*? Without a careful *target market* definition it is extraordinarily easy to waste advertising money abroad.

Once the target market has been defined, media planning can begin. This can be done in one of two ways:

(*i*) *Direct from London*—via overseas media U.K. representatives' offices. Almost all press media throughout the world are represented in London, and can be traced through the *Advertisers' Annual Trade Directory* which comprehensively lists overseas media specialists. While booking in the major foreign newspapers and magazines can be made quite effectively in this way, it is rarely satisfactory to try to book space from London in the smaller local or trade journals; nor can television, radio, cinema, posters or other national media be properly booked in this way. However, the truly international publications (*Time, Newsweek, Playboy, Readers' Digest*) can certainly be booked in London—or in New York, Paris, Frankfurt, Sydney etc . . .

(*ii*) *Through a local agency*—This may be either the local office of one of the major international advertising agencies. J. Walter Thompson, McCann Erickson, Young and Rubicam, Ogilvy and Mather, and Lintas own offices throughout the world, though inevitably each agency is stronger in some areas and weaker in others; alternatively booking may be through the local affiliate or associate of a U.K. agency—all the top fifty British advertising agencies have trading partners in different parts of the world, and can set up additional partnerships in new localities with their opposite numbers overseas as and when necessary.

Here we must return to our earlier distinction between multi-national companies and national companies selling abroad. Multi-national companies are more likely to use an international (or multi-national) advertising agency; their own local organisation will then work with the local executives of the main agency throughout the world, and will often have a good measure of local autonomy, whereas a national company looking for exports through sales agents is unlikely to have its own executives operating permanently in each territory, and will therefore seek to control marketing and advertising more closely from its headquarters.

Creative problems

The first question to be asked of a proposed international campaign is: will the creative ideas travel? Will a campaign that has proved successful in Britain or the U.S.A. be equally successful in Australia or New Zealand—where the language is the same but social and marketing conditions are quite different? More difficult still, will it translate into German, French, Italian or Spanish and still retain its impact and its relevance? Such imponderable questions can only be answered for each campaign individually. However, there are definite guidelines to be followed when the problem is attacked.

(*a*) *Local adaptation*—Except in those infrequent occasions when circumstances make it unavoidable, advertisements should never be created in the headquarters' country and placed direct without comment, interpretation and if necessary adaptation by the local agency. Delicacy must be employed, since local operators frequently seek to change whatever has been sent to them simply for change's sake. But if they can advance sound and sensible arguments for their amendments, then these must be accepted.

(*b*) *Local translation*—More essential still, if the advertising is to appear in another language it must be translated locally (and not at headquarters). It must be translated by bilingual advertising professionals, usually copywriters, and not by translation agencies or interpreters. The brief must be to translate the sense, the creative communications objective, and not the pedantic literal meaning. Once translated, the headquarters office must have it translated back again into its original tongue as a simple check that the original translation was carried out accurately.

(*c*) *Local testing*—If there is any possibility (and there usually is) that the strategy or tone of the advertising may not be absolutely right for the particular market, it should *always* be tested, getting a local research company to use the techniques described in Chapter 6. The testing of an international campaign in its local situation can do more than avoid the foolish waste of money; it can avoid the aggravation of chauvinistic sensitivities which can create ill-will and

cause lasting harm to any company seeking to trade beyond
its own frontiers.

International campaigns: pros and cons

Why should anybody even wish to run a universal campaign
in every country rather than let each of them produce its
own advertising for its own market, to the best of its ability?
The worst, but often the most truthful answer to this question is: tidiness. Many business executives have an innate
and normally well-founded distaste for disorganisation;
running a dozen different advertising campaigns in different countries for exactly the same product offers at first
sight an appearance of total chaos. But the understandable
desire for tidiness is not a sufficient reason for running a
homogeneous international campaign. Here are other, more
soundly based reasons:

1. A campaign that has proved successful in one country
has a high likelihood of success in another.
2. If the product is the same, the probability is that its sales
advantages will be the same.
3. Outside the U.S. and U.K., advertising skills are often
less advanced, and locally developed advertising can sometimes be embarrassingly amateurish and ineffective.
4. To an ever-increasing extent people, particularly businessmen, travel abroad, and will see the product's advertising everywhere they go.
5. International campaigns minimise the time-costs of top
management involvement in advertising decisions.
6. Production costs, particularly of expensive photography
and commercials, can be amortised and kept to a minimum.

None of these advantages will weigh heavily in the balance
if the international advertising is genuinely wrong for any
particular local market. But with the above advantages
greatly weighted in favour of international advertising (for
international brands) the onus must rest with the local

management to prove by means of testing, if they believe it to be the case, that the international campaign will not work for them.

Controls and remuneration

As can easily be understood, the placing of campaigns in other countries, at hundreds and sometimes thousands of miles' distance, can be difficult to control. (We are not talking here about legal or voluntary controls on advertising content, which is a separate though highly important subject, since most countries now have legislation circumscribing advertising to a greater or lesser degree, but of the control exerted on an overseas campaign by the advertiser and agency at headquarters.)

As before, there are two main aspects to this problem:

Advertising placed direct—In this case the *content* of the advertisement is directly under the control of the headquarters' office, and the problem is to control the local media. When messages and pieces of paper travel long distances they are frequently misinterpreted on arrival. The golden rules are (*i*) to keep the instructions short, absolutely clear and translate them if there is the slightest chance of misunderstanding; and (*ii*) to insist that free *voucher* copies of all media carrying advertisements are sent back for close checking before any invoice for advertising is paid. Regrettably, small foreign journals are notoriously bad at sending in such voucher copies unless they are firmly insisted upon and payment is delayed until they arrive.

Advertising placed through local agencies—Here, generally, the boot is entirely on the other foot. The local agency can be relied upon to supervise and control media bookings (and if it does not do this efficiently, then another local agency should be found). The control problem in this case is more commonly that the local agency, encouraged by the local office of the client, will seek to alter the *creative* content of the advertising. The pros and cons of this have already been discussed, and we are assuming here that a clear decision on the matter has been taken. In this case the responsibility lies firmly with the advertiser's head office to communicate this decision in unmistakable terms both to the local executives and to the local agency; and thereafter to ensure that the decision is implemented.

All this co-ordination and control will of course involve considerable effort, time and money. Airmail letters and parcels, overseas telephone calls, telegrams, telexes and, most expensive of all, overseas travel, can together quickly build up into hideous (all too often unforeseen) total costs. Before such costs are incurred it is essential for the advertiser to prepare a realistic budget for the operation, with a healthy sum set aside for contingencies. From the advertising agency's point of view, handling international advertising can easily become a loss-making business, particularly if commissions have to be split with a local agency, as is the usual practice. To obtain a reasonable revenue from international accounts, therefore, agencies normally agree with their clients that they should be paid an extra 5% commission, i.e. 20% in total. This is then split 10%–10% between the headquarters agency and the local agency. Alternatively the agencies may work on a time-cost fee basis. Either way, heavy out-of-pocket expenses such as air fares will normally be charged separately to clients, at cost.

International advertising, then, may not be quite as glamorous as at first it sounds. In fact it demands infinite and painstaking attention to detail—foreign media sizes and reproduction methods, timing, currencies and floating exchange rates, imprecise translation and inaccurate market data are all snares in which the unwary may be caught. But despite all the possible pitfalls, once you have mastered it, it is both stimulating and fun.

Advertising in Communist bloc countries

Hitherto, Western exporters have undertaken almost no advertising in Communist bloc countries; and such advertising would probably not be acceptable in those countries most hostile to Western economic practices, such as Albania. There can be no starker visual display of the effects of advertising on urban appearances than a trip across the border between West and East Berlin.

However, times are changing, and commercial advertising is already a growing feature of several of the Communist economies. Studies of the nature and extent of consumer advertising in the Soviet Union, Poland, Hungary and Yugoslavia (see Bibliography) suggest that where central control of economic planning loosens, and demand and supply are not rigidly and forcefully correlated, there is rapidly seen to be a need for advertising. The Communist hierarchies are not implacably opposed to consumer advertising, though there is a strong movement against what are believed to be persuasive, emotional advertisements and in favour of factual informative ones.

In Moscow an organisation called *Vneshtorgreklama* functions similarly to a Western advertising agency; in Warsaw *Agpol* and in Zagreb *Czeha* (particularly this last, which has its own television and photographic studio and acts, for example, for Pepsi-Cola in Yugoslavia) are extremely similar to Western full-service agencies. Perhaps J. Walter Thompson and McCann Erickson will have Moscow offices in the near future!

Think Exercises

1. 'The world is shrinking all the time.'
   'Nonsense. Nationalism and chauvinism have never been stronger.'
   How does the international advertiser cope with these apparently contradictory propositions?

2. Think of five product fields, other than those mentioned in the chapter, where British consumers behave broadly similarly to other European consumers; then think of another five fields which are peculiarly British in character.

3. The overriding problem in international business, people are fond of saying, is personal *communications*. Think of *all* the communications media that an International Marketing Director can use in his personal communications (e.g. letter, telephone etc.) and then list advantages and disadvantages of each of them.

9

Advertising and the Economy

We have laid great emphasis upon the heterogeneity of advertising, on the many different kinds of advertising and the diverse ways in which it functions. It is time to finish the book with a look at a subject which is given scant attention in many economics textbooks: the overall role and function of advertising in the economy.

Advertising—supply and demand

The economic role of advertising can be analysed in terms of its supply and demand. The media supply advertising, for which they charge. Advertisers have a demand for advertising, for which they are willing to pay a price. For both parties advertising can be thought of in economic terms as one of the many commodities which they buy and sell.

From the point of view of the media advertising is, as we have seen, one of their prime sources of income. The percentage of total income attributable to advertising varies from medium to medium. It accounts for 98 % of ITV's revenue (the remaining 2 % coming from sales of programmes, which in turn could not have been produced without the advertising finance); for national newspapers and magazines the percentage varies from approximately 30 % to a maximum of 100 % for free sheets; in the cinema the percentage is significantly lower and nowadays generally runs at less than 5 %. Advertising of course supports commercial radio and contributes revenue to such diverse bodies as

British Rail, London Transport, the Post Office (via direct mail), the hotel industry (via exhibitions and conventions) and even the Central Electricity Generating Board (via illuminated signs). In each case advertising, being an element of increased revenue, allows them to reduce—marginally or totally—the charge they make to the ultimate consumer of their products.

The price that media charge for advertising is dependent upon three economic factors: costs, supply and demand. These determine what economists call the *price elasticity of supply*. Costs include both the cost of producing the advertising and the cost of producing the media themselves. For example, newspapers estimate that approximately 50% of the price they charge for advertising goes in paper, ink,

labour and other administrative costs. (The remaining 50 %
is 'profit' and goes towards the cost of producing the paper
itself.) Likewise for direct mail, most of the advertising cost
goes directly into the cost of producing, printing and posting
the advertising material.

On the other hand, in the case of television, and still more
so in the case of radio, the marginal cost of transmitting
advertisements (once the station exists) is negligible. In
theory, transmitting companies could accept more and more
advertising, with almost no effect upon their costs. (This is
why U.S. television carries so many commercials and why
in the U.K. the total time allotted to advertising has been
limited by legislation.) Clearly the television and radio
stations need to charge rates that will generate sufficient
revenue for them to transmit programmes which will
attract viewers and listeners. But once those costs have been
met the price of television advertising is determined almost
purely by the classic market forces of supply and demand.
In summary then: all media determine what they charge
for advertising in the light of—

(*i*) Their costs;
(*ii*) The supply of advertising they can make available;
(*iii*) Their judgement of what advertisers are willing
and able to pay.

This brings us to the other half of the economic equation:
the demand for advertising and the price which advertisers
are prepared to pay for it (in economists' terms: the *price
elasticity of demand*). This is more difficult to analyse in economic terms than the price elasticity of supply, primarily
because the total number of advertisers is far greater than
the number of media, and the benefits they seek from
advertising are both more various and more complex.
(Media generally speaking seek money, pure and simple,
from advertising.)

Let us remind ourselves of the seven faces of advertising:

Manufacturers' consumer advertising
Retailer advertising
Trade, technical and industrial advertising
Financial advertising
Recruitment advertising
Classified advertising
Government and public service advertising

It will readily be seen that the function of advertising varies from 'face' to 'face'. More importantly, their *dependence* upon advertising varies widely. We could all live without announcing our family births, marriages and deaths in the classified columns; whereas many consumer goods companies, and estate agents, and car dealers and other commercial companies would suffer a marked contraction of their business if they could not advertise their goods to their publics. This in turn would lead to inefficient distribution, unprofitability and eventually unemployment.

Retailers use advertising to increase store traffic, and are thus able to amortise their overheads, lower their prices and accept lower profit margins. Trade, technical and industrial companies are often less dependent upon advertising than are many other types of business, but nevertheless rely upon it to increase the efficiency, and lower the costs, of their sales and distributive organisations. Both financial and recruitment advertisers use it to reach, as cheaply as possible, specific minority groups. The government uses advertising both for their recruitment—in which role, as Lord Kitchener discovered in World War I, it is virtually indispensable—and for public services, in which role it has been found often to be more cost-effective than any other means of mass-communication and persuasion.

Each advertiser decides for himself whether the rates media are charging for advertising space and time are economic. The decision, as we have seen, can rarely be based upon strictly *scientific* analysis. Very few economic decisions are strictly scientific. Advertisers investigate all the data available, and then spend their money in the media if they feel that the end results will be worthwhile, however this may be measured. (Nobody spends money on advertising or on anything else, unless they believe that in exchange they are obtaining something they require.)

Periodically you may read in the newspapers that advertising rates have risen and that certain advertisers no longer think it economic to buy space or time. Their withdrawal from advertising will, in due course, force the media to rebalance the equation; and the price of advertising—like that of other commodities—will thus be determined by the forces of supply and demand.

Advertising, efficiency and choice

Clearly it is possible for an economy to run, albeit less efficiently, with little or no advertising: Communist bloc countries produce little advertising even today.

The question we must ask is: advertising involves the utilisation of economic resources—what benefits are obtained in return? This complicated subject, like many of the others we have touched upon in the preceding 250 pages, demands a book to itself. One of the prime aims of this Teach Yourself book has been to stimulate your interest for further exploration of the fascinating world of advertising. Here we can but state briefly the three basic economic benefits that society reaps from the advertising it produces:

1. The distribution of goods and services is achieved more cheaply and more quickly than could possibly be the case if advertising were curtailed.
2. Manufacturers produce and offer to the public a far wider choice of goods and services than they possibly could if advertising were not available to them.
3. Advertising stimulates competition, innovation and economic growth.

In short, advertising increases economic efficiency, freedom of choice, and society's wealth: a very fair return for an investment of 1%–2% of most countries' Gross National Product.

10

Careers and Qualifications

'I went in to see my Uncle Joe one evening after work. I hadn't been in advertising long. He asked me how I had spent my day.

It had been a day like any other in advertising—atypical. There had been a recording session. Fifteen takes before all of us thought the announcer had got it right. I had also written a leaflet for a garage, checked numerous proofs and done some lasting damage to a jingle.

I explained all this in considerable detail. I waited. My uncle, a tailor long left Poland, looked at me. After a pause he said:

'For *this* you went to Oxford?'

He wasn't so much asking a question as telling me something. And what could I tell him? It is difficult to convey the satisfaction one gets out of advertising, the stimulus, the intellectual and emotional involvement with other people's products and yet other people's behaviour and response to those products.'

This is the opening of *Creative Advertising*,* an excellent book on how advertising works by David Bernstein, who worked as creative director of three major agencies before founding *The Creative Business* which is now one of Britain's leading product development consultancies. It neatly summarises many of the joys and sorrows of a job in advertising.

* *Creative Advertising*, David Bernstein (Longman), 1974.

There are three stages at which it is possible to enter advertising:

> Direct from school, with 'O' or 'A' levels.
> From university, as a graduate.
> Later in life, from another career.

Opportunities exist at all three stages, and in all three sectors of the advertising industry—with an advertiser, with the media or with an advertising agency. There are about 150 different career opportunities in advertising and by now you must yourself have a reasonably clear picture of the differing nature of the job functions in each sector of the business. If you are seriously considering a career in advertising you should know which type of job you would like most and which you would probably be best at.

However, you have learned that advertising is a fairly small business in which only a modest number of people are employed. This in turn means that comparatively few new people are recruited into it each year, so that unless you are

exceptionally fortunate you will need to put in many job applications before you are successful. You will need to be determined, persistent and resilient, and you may have initially to accept a job that would not necessarily have been your first choice, so that you can zig-zag your way towards your ultimate ambition as you accumulate experience and contacts.

Getting your first advertising job

As with most other jobs the first step is to write a letter to your prospective employer(s) attaching to it your *curriculum vitae* (CV)—a résumé which succinctly marshalls together all the facts about you that the employer will want to know:

> Who are you?
> What have you done?
> What do you know?
> What can you do?
> What kind of job do you want?
> Why are you interested in advertising?
> What spare time are you willing to spend on training yourself for an advertising career?

If you have already taken the trouble to register as a student with the CAM Education Foundation (see below), or better still have already started an advertising training course, it will prove that you are serious in your approach and demonstrate your commitment to an advertising career. Above all, when preparing your *curriculum vitae* try hard to put yourself in the employer's place and include the facts that if you were he you would like to know. Not too many, not too few, but all that are relevant. (A good *curriculum vitae* is unlikely to be shorter than one fully-typed A4 page or longer than two A4 pages.)

No sensible employer minds if a CV has been photocopied or duplicated. Everybody realises that an aspiring entrant into advertising will need to make many job applications.

The covering letter which accompanies the CV should, however, be individually written or typed. This is firstly a matter of politeness, and secondly shows that you are prepared to make a particular, personal effort for the employer concerned. The immediate object of the letter is to get yourself interviewed. (You will never be employed by post, as it were, on the basis of your letter plus CV alone.) Your

letter must therefore be directly aimed at interesting the employer sufficiently to make him want to meet you. Make the letter simple, direct and economical. If you can be interesting and original so much the better; but do avoid at all costs being flippant, coy, cute or facetious. Humorous letters—especially for jobs—are exceptionally difficult to write. Yet an astonishingly large number of people try, and their letters are almost always embarassing.

If your letter has succeeded you will be granted an interview. Plan for it carefully. Try to find out about the company: the *Advertiser's Annual Trade Directory* will almost certainly be of help. Think out in advance why you believe you would be suitable for the job and for the company; at the same time think of any questions you would like to ask the interviewer to help you make up *your* mind that the job is the right one. Remember that an interview is a two-way process. An employer will expect you to want to find out everything about the job that might be relevant to you, so don't be afraid to ask questions.

When you land your first offer of a job in advertising, remember that initial salary is of considerably less importance than the opportunities for future progress that the job can open to you. Long gone are the days when a beginner would need to accept a job in the J. Walter Thompson mail room without pay, for the privilege of being allowed to get into that agency at all. You will rightly expect to start with a living wage—but not much more. It will be after your first two or three salary increases that you will discover that a career in advertising can be financially rewarding as well as (to use David Bernstein's words) satisfying, stimulating and involving.

Education for Advertising: CAM

Since 1970 education for advertising has been centralised under the responsibility of a body called the Communication Advertising and Marketing Education Foundation Limited, usually known simply as CAM. CAM is backed and sponsored by all branches of the advertising industry including:

> The Advertising Association
> Incorporated Society of British Advertisers
> Institute of Practitioners in Advertising
> Institute of Public Relations
> Incorporated Advertising Managers Association

As you can see, CAM qualifications are highly regarded throughout all spheres of advertising. CAM offers two levels of qualification: the CAM Certificate in Communications Studies, and the more advanced CAM Diploma. The qualification Dip.CAM commands great respect throughout U.K. advertising and marketing and indeed throughout the world.

Outline of scheme

The CAM Certificate in Communications Studies is awarded after the first part of the course (normally two years) on the basis of examinations designed to establish that candidates have a practical and basic knowledge of the six Certificate subjects. These are Advertising, Marketing, Public Relations, Media, Research and Behavioural Studies, and Communications.

The CAM Diploma involves one more year of study after the Certificate stage. This final year is planned to deal with practical aspects of the subjects based largely on case-studies. These are designed to test ability to handle real-life situations and all examiners are senior practitioners looking for a professional grasp of essentials and the ability to deal competently with the questions they have posed.

At present CAM Diplomas are awarded in Advertising, Public Relations, Media and Creative Studies.

Entry requirements

Students are required to be at least eighteen years old and to meet one of the following four criteria:

1. Five GCE passes in relevant subjects, one of which must be at 'A' Level;
2. OND or ONC in Business Studies;
3. To have been in full-time employment in any part of the communications business for a minimum of one year: *and* to have five GCE passes at 'O' Level in relevant subjects;
4. In special circumstances, students, who have been 'in the business' for at least three years, can be accepted with lesser

academic qualifications, providing they have the commendation of their employer or college principal.

Courses leading to the CAM Certificate and Diploma are offered in the major population centres of the U.K.* listed below and in a number of overseas centres.

Central London
College for the Distributive Trades
City of London Polytechnic

Greater London

Croydon	Croydon Technical College
Ealing	Ealing School of Art and Photography
	Ealing Technical College
Romford	Barking College of Technology, Romford
Twickenham	Twickenham College of Technology
Watford	Watford College of Technology
	Watford School of Art

Colleges outside London area

Birmingham	Matthew Boulton Technical College
Bournemouth	Bournemouth and Poole College
Bradford	Bradford College of Art and Technology
Bristol	Bristol Polytechnic
Darlington	Darlington College of Technology
Edinburgh	Stevenson College of Further Education
Glasgow	Central College of Commerce
Leeds	Park Lane College of Further Education
Luton	Barnfield College, School of Art and Design

* Subject to numbers registering for the course.

Manchester	Manchester Polytechnic
Newcastle	Newcastle-Upon-Tyne Polytechnic
Norwich	Norwich City College
Nottingham	Trent Polytechnic
Reading	Berkshire College of Art & Design, Reading
Salford	Salford College of Technology
Southampton	Southampton College of Art
Stockport	Stockport College of Technology
Wolverhampton	Wulfrun College of Further Education
Worksop	North Nottinghamshire College of Further Education
York	York College of Further Education

Correspondence courses

International Correspondence Schools, Intertext House, Stewarts Road, London, SW8 4UJ.

Metropolitan College, Aldermaston Court, Reading, Berks.

The address of CAM is: Abford House, 15, Wilton Road, London, SW1V 7NJ. Tel: 01-828 7506

Higher National Certificate or Diploma in Business Studies (Advertising/Marketing)

An alternative qualification to the final CAM Diploma is the Higher National Certificate in Business Studies (Advertising and Marketing). Within the Business Studies examination structure, it is important for the student to select the Advertising and Marketing options, as alternatives are not acceptable. The Higher National Certificate is a two-year part-time course, and three subjects must be taken in each year.

(The Higher National Diploma is a full-time two-year course or a three-year sandwich course of which about half the time is spent in industry or commerce. The Diploma is only granted when a student can prove twelve months of business or administrative experience: therefore students who complete the two-year Diploma course must wait a further year before receiving their Diplomas.)

Basic requirements for the Higher National Certificate are:

(*i*) Two approved subjects at A-Level; minimum age, 18. *Or*
(*ii*) Ordinary National Certificate in Business Studies (a two-year part-time course for students at least 16 years old and with at least four O-Level subjects). *Or*
(*iii*) Students over 21, or with two A-Levels in subjects not 'approved' for business studies may take a year's conversion course (part-time) in Economics, Accounting and Law to qualify for HNC. In exceptional cases, students of 25 and over may be admitted direct to an HNC course.

Higher National Certificate: Year 1
Applied Economics
Advertising I (Administration and Media)
Advertising II (Advertisement Design, Printing and Production, Copywriting).

Higher National Certificate: Year 2
Applied Economics
Marketing
Market Research

Other advertising courses

Diploma in Communication Studies
The Polytechnic of Central London offers a full-time course over three academic years leading to a Diploma in Communication Studies. It includes the study of an academic subject at a degree level for three years; a co-ordinated study of the theory of communication for three years; practical work in journalism, sound radio, television and advertising in the first two years and a special study of one medium in the final year. The course is designed to help the student

discover his or her particular interests and abilities before choosing a specialisation for the third year.

Basic requirements
The minimum age of entry is 18. Students should have passed five subjects in the General Certificate of Education including at least two at A-Level. An entrance examination and interview is held in May.

Subjects
Either Contemporary Literature or Modern History (three years); The Theory and Practice of Communication (three years); final year specialisation chosen from Public Relations, Sound Radio, Advertising, Television, Audio-Visual Aids, Publishing.

Important professional bodies

On several occasions earlier in the book reference has been made to the various professional and trade organisations within advertising and its associated industries. All of these organisations are most willing to give help and advice to students and certain of them—particularly the Advertising Association and the Institute of Practitioners in Advertising —have excellent libraries which students may use freely. Here then is a list of the main professional bodies within advertising and marketing:

The Advertising Association
The Advertising Association, which was founded in 1926, today represents all sides of the advertising business and is thus the leading organisation within the industry. All the other sectional bodies—those representing advertisers, media, agencies etc.—are affiliated to it and provide its revenue via a levy upon their funds. The Association compiles and publishes all the basic statistics on advertising in the U.K., and is the body with which govermental and civil service institutions will normally deal when matters concerning advertising arise.

Address: The Advertising Association, Abford House, Wilton Road, London, S.W.1.
Telephone: 01-828 2771

The Institute of Practitioners in Advertising
The Institute of Practitioners in Advertising (IPA) is the trade association representing Britain's advertising agencies and the professional institute for those people employed in them. Approximately 300 agencies are in membership of the IPA, and these place between them at least 90 % of all U.K. advertising. The IPA provides comprehensive data and statistics for agency managements on agency revenues, costs and profits. For individuals within agencies the IPA Society provides an extremely lively social and educational calendar of events each year.

Address: The Institute of Practitioners in Advertising, 44 Belgrave Square, London, S.W.1.
Telephone: 01-235 7020

The Incorporated Society of British Advertisers (ISBA) was formed over seventy years ago under the name of the Advertisers' Protection Society. This name, dropped after its first twenty years of existence, indicates to this day the prime role of the Society: to promote and protect the advertising and marketing interests of all who use advertising above or below the line. ISBA's members are responsible for well over 50 % of the country's annual advertising expenditures, and it is able to draw upon all of its members' wide experience of commerce and industry.

Address: Incorporated Society of British Advertisers, 2 Basil Street, London, S.W.1.
Telephone: 01-584 522

The Institute of Marketing
The Institute of Marketing has over 16,000 members spread throughout agencies, advertisers, media and market research companies. Its principal aims, as the leading professional

marketing organisation in the U.K., are to make the principles and practices of marketing more widely known and effectively practised. To this end a full-scale all-the-year-round programme of educational courses and seminars is run at the Institute's own College of Marketing, which was established in 1958 to conduct both residential and non-residential courses in marketing management.

Address: The Institute of Marketing, Moor Hall, Cookham, Berkshire.
Telephone: Bourne End (062 85) 24922

The Market Research Society

The Market Research Society (MRS), founded in 1947, is the incorporated professional body for those working in market research with research companies or as market researchers within industry and advertising agencies. With over 2,000 members it is now the largest body of its kind anywhere in the world. The MRS publishes a Standard Code of Practice to which all members must adhere; this covers professional ethics and standard conditions for conducting sample surveys and reporting results. On behalf of its profession the MRS maintains liaison with government departments, universities, scientific institutions and other organisations both in the U.K. and abroad.

Address: Market Research Society, 15 Belgrave Square, London, S.W.1.
Telephone: 01-235 4709

The Institute of Public Relations

The Institute of Public Relations was founded in 1948 by a group of public relations officers from government, commerce and industry, to represent the interests of their rapidly expanding profession. Today the Institute has a membership approaching 3,000 and its main objects are to promote the development of public relations and to encourage high professional standards. The Institute also organises educational activities in PR, principally in liaison with CAM.

Address: Institute of Public Relations, 1 Great James Street, London, W.C.1.
Telephone: 01-405 5505

With this chapter we shall cease to set Think Exercises— first, because this and the remaining chapters do not lend themselves to Think Exercises; but second, and more importantly, because you are now sufficiently knowledge- able about advertising to tackle more specific advertising problems. To this end you will find a selection of questions from recent CAM Certificate Examinations on pages 267 to 273 and these will give you a good idea of the CAM Certificate level.

Appendix 1

International Comparisons

Expenditure in US $ (millions)

	Advertising Expenditure as a Percentage of Gross National Product %	TOTAL	Press and Magazines	Posters and Outdoor	Cinema	Radio	TV	Other
Austria	0·35	342·6	120·2	10·2	1·4	18·0	45·1	147·7
Belgium	0·50	276·9	151·5	42·4	4·4	2·1	2·8*	73·7
Denmark	0·48	355·3	212·6	5·5	3·3	—*	—*	133·9
Finland	0·78	256·9	136·0	6·9	1·1	—*	26·9	86·0
France	0·39	1981·7	668·1	25·1	25·1	98·2	142·1	993·1
Italy	0·40	942·8	469·4	62·6	33·0	75·9	125·0	176·9
Netherlands	0·70	771·8	462·4	26·7	3·3	6·1	57·6	215·7
Norway	0·58	178·2	139·1	4·6	3·6	—*	—*	30·9
Spain	0·52	753·1	351·8	53·4	14·2	34·7	128·1	170·9
Sweden	0·40	506·0	253·0	12·7	7·6	—*	—*	232·7
Switzerland	0·70	744·2	303·8	41·8	6·2	—*	31·8	361·2
U.K.	0·80	2,215·0	1,512·9	81·3	19·1	14·3	485·2	102·2
U.S.A.	1·24	26,780·0	10,477·0	345·0	†	1,837·0	4,851·0	9,270·0
W. Germany	0·90	2,523·1	1,565·8	108·0	22·2	85·2	290·6	451·3

* Media not available for advertising; where figure is quoted, this is overlap advertising from nearby countries.

† Included in 'Other'.

Sources: AA/IPA

N.B. The high figure for 'Other' in many countries outside of the U.K. is accounted for by the fact that different countries include different items—e.g. exhibitions, catalogues etc.—in the compilation of advertising statistics.

Appendix 2

CAM examination questions

The qualifications for obtaining the CAM Certificate (see page 257) normally include two years' study, and the CAM Diploma calls for a further year's studentship thereafter. Thus nobody could be expected to be able to pass the CAM Certificate and Diploma examinations merely on the basis of having read this book. Nevertheless, this book (which is recommended by CAM) covers a good deal of the CAM Syllabus, and if you have mastered the contents you will be well on the way towards being able to answer many of the questions set in CAM (and HNC) Examination Papers.

Here is a selection of over thirty questions from recent papers, which you can use to test yourself:

Advertising general

1. 'The general aim of advertising is to increase profitable sales, but other specific objectives are of importance.'

   Discuss this statement, and identify five specific objectives which might be incorporated into an advertising programme.

2. During the first visit of the Advertising Manager of a prospective client he asks you to describe the structure and work flow of your medium-sized agency.

   (*i*) Explain the structure and the function of each department;
   (*ii*) Briefly describe the stages that a new campaign would go through from initiation to implementation.

3. A rabid and rhetorical critic of advertising publishes an article in a newspaper in which, among other things, he makes the following assertion: 'The trouble with advertisers is that they are

largely ill-disciplined and are permitted by our society to operate either outside or within the fringes of the law. They will, of course, tell you about their vaunted system of voluntary control, but we all know that this system is entirely without the essential teeth of legal sanctions. What those of us who care for the consumer want today, is a determined programme of legislation to enclose advertising, for the first time, in a strict framework of legal control.'.

Write a short, pithy article in reply.

4. Describe briefly the methods which may be used to determine the level of the advertising budget, and state any problems which could be encountered in their use. Make a recommendation for the one you prefer.

5. 'My advertising appropriation represents 10% of my overheads; by cutting it to 5% I can increase my net profit.'

Choose a product or service and then discuss this statement in the context of the example you have selected.

6. 'Recent governments have placed consumer affairs high on their list of priorities and pressure for further statutory controls on advertising seems likely to increase. The voluntary control system has worked satisfactorily in the past and since the industry is self-policing, further legislative control is unnecessary.' Discuss.

7. You are the Advertising Manager of Blows Heaters Ltd., the leading manufacturer of industrial and domestic heaters in the U.K. Market conditions have changed in the last two years and competition has increased.

Write a brief to your Managing Director defining the type of agency you would recommend to spend an appropriation of £100,000 per annum, the size and character of that agency, and the exact range of services for which you would be searching.

8. Your London agency has prepared recommendations for the launch of your product (a new furniture polish) in all of the EEC countries. They strongly favour central control from London in all creative work and media selection. Discuss the advantages and disadvantages of this recommendation.

Media

1. Imagine that you live in an ideal world. List, under paragraph headings, the information you would require in the media brief to enable you to prepare a media recommendation and media plan, and explain how you would use the information under each paragraph head.

2. Discuss for what product categories and target audience you would recommend the use of 4-sheet posters in shopping precincts. Justify this selection in relation to local radio.

3. As media director of an agency which has just landed a European consumer account, you have been asked to provide client with an outline of media facilities in the United Kingdom market.

   Write a memorandum for your new client.

4. Explain the role of the following organisations:

   (*i*) Audit Bureau of Circulation
   (*ii*) Advertising Association
   (*iii*) Independent Broadcasting Authority
   (*iv*) Evening Newspaper Advertising Bureau

5. Three of the main sources of media information currently available to the media department are as follows:

   (*i*) JICNARS
   (*ii*) JICTAR
   (*iii*) TGI

   Describe the basic information contained in any two of the above. Give sample size, method of data collection, regularity of issue, media and markets covered, definitions used and post-survey analysis facilities offered.

6. Describe the main characteristics of four of the following types of media:

   (*i*) National Daily Newspapers
   (*ii*) Women's Weekly Magazines
   (*iii*) Provincial Daily Newspapers
   (*iv*) Commercial Television
   (*v*) Commercial Radio
   (*vi*) Trade and Technical Magazines

Detail the broad advantages and disadvantages of the media selected, and give estimates of current costs and coverage levels.

7. What is a JICTAR TV homes rating?
   Describe the research system which provides this kind of information.

8. Describe the main characteristics of five of the following types of media. Include details of costs and coverage, as well as any advantages and disadvantages to an advertiser.

   (*i*) National Daily Newspapers
   (*ii*) Women's Weekly Magazines
   (*iii*) Provincial Evening Newspapers
   (*iv*) Trade and Technical Magazines
   (*v*) Television
   (*vi*) Posters
   (*vii*) Commercial Radio

9. Discuss the advantages and disadvantages of the use of the cinema as an advertising medium. Include details of methods of booking, approximate costs, coverage and measurement of cinema audiences.

Marketing

1. Opportunities in a market increase when the seller recognises that it is made up of many parts. In what way can markets be segmented? Illustrate your answer with examples.

2. A fundamental question to be asked of any product or service is 'To whom are we selling?' Discuss the importance of this question with particular reference to the problems of identifying prospects for both advertising and personal selling.

3. You have been asked to talk to a group of intelligent housewives on the subject 'What is Marketing?' You have been warned that a vocal minority is ready to argue that marketing is primarily concerned with techniques of persuasion. Prepare notes of the points you will be making to answer the question posed in the title and disarm your critics.

Research

1. In recent years a considerable sum of money has been devoted to trying to reduce injuries and death to car drivers and front-seat passengers by persuading them to wear their seat belts. (You may well have noted the 'Clunk-Click' campaign.)

   In 1975 a large budget has been set aside for the continuation of this campaign. You have been asked to present proposals for monitoring its effectiveness in changing motorists' attitudes to road safety and in persuading them and their passengers to use seat belts for every journey. What research would you recommend? (You may assume that the advertising is mainly on TV, with six-week bursts of concentrated activity followed by six weeks of no more than 'support' advertising in the press and on posters. You may also assume that a generous research budget is available.)

2. What are the advantages and disadvantages of collecting product purchasing data on a consumer panel, and what are the main uses of such data?

3. Interviewer bias is a serious problem in market research. Identify its main sources. Outline the steps that you would expect a responsible research agency to take to minimise its effects.

4. Your agency is handling the launch of a major deodorant. The first year's advertising has been judged so important that two campaigns have been developed. One finished TV commercial has been made for each campaign. Each commercial adopts quite a different advertising approach as well as differing in treatment. You have to devise pre-testing research which will help your client decide which campaign to use. What are your recommendations?

5. Your company has been invited to submit outline proposals to a company marketing tights, stockings and a full range of underwear for setting up continuous research on the total market and providing data by garment, style, brand price and retail outlet. Discuss your basic reasons for advocating either retail auditing or a consumer diary panel with particular references to the importance of data that only one or the other method can provide. (You may ignore detailed considerations of relative cost.)

Production

1. Give the advantages and disadvantages of each of the following in relation to each other:

    (*i*) Letterpress
    (*ii*) Offset Litho
    (*iii*) Sheetfed gravure
    (*iv*) Silkscreen

2. There is a sequence of operations in the production of a press advertisement between the client's approval of a layout and the final appearance of the advertisement in a number of newspapers. Give an account of the stages involved.

3. Assume that you have been asked to give a talk to a group of trainees on 'The four main printing processes—their principles and usage.' Prepare a set of lecture notes for your talk, giving references for examples of usage.

4. Compare the advantages and disadvantages of VTR against colour film for the following: location shots, editing, speed, colour fidelity.

Copy and Design

1. From a copy of *Woman's Own* choose any full-page or larger advertisement which you think is unsuccessful and:

    (*i*) Explain why you think it is unsuccessful.
    (*ii*) Write down what you take to be the target audience and the advertising objective of the advertisement.
    (*iii*) Rewrite the advertisement as you think it should have been written.
    (*iv*) Explain how you think the Art Director should set it out in terms of layout, illustration and typography.

2. Comment on any TV commercial or series of commercials which in your opinion show an especially effective use of each of the following:

    (*i*) A sung message or jingle
    (*ii*) Cartoon animation
    (*iii*) Testimonial endorsement or celebrity association.

NB. Questions set in the CAM Copy and Design examination often either refer to well-known campaigns current at the time, or include advertisements for comment which are attached to the test paper.

Appendix 3

Bibliography and Reading List

* Recommended by CAM

Advertising—General

Advertising in Perspective (Advertising Association, 1974)
* Advertising Today, F. Jefkins (Intertext Books, 1976)
Madison Avenue U.S.A., M. Mayer (Penguin, 1958)
* Advertising Made Simple, F. Jefkins (W. H. Allen, 1973)
What Advertising Does (IPA Booklet, 1976)
* What Advertising Is, M. Smelt (Pelham Press, 1972)
* Industrial Publicity, N. A. Hart (Associated Business Programmes, 1973)

Marketing

* Developing New Brands, S. King (Pitman, 1973)
* Innovations in Marketing (T. Levitt) (Pan Books, 1962)
* How to do Business in Branded Goods, E. Morgan (Longman, 1972)
* Marketing, C. McIver (Business Books for IPA, 1964)
* Offensive Marketing, J. H. Davidson (Cassell and Co., 1972)
Mail Order Marketing, E. Ornstein (Gower Press, 1970)

Media

* Advertising Media & Campaign Planning, A. Swindells (Butterworths, 1966)
* Media Planning, J. R. Adams (Business Books for IPA, 1970)
* Spending Advertising Money, S. Broadbent (Business Books, 1975)

Agencies, Creative and Communications
* Confessions of an Advertising Man, D. Ogilvy (Longman, 1963)
  Creative Advertising, D. Bernstein (Longman, 1974)
* Copywriting, P. Stobo (Business Books, 1967)
* Reality in Advertising, R. Reeves (Alfred Knops, New York, 1961)
* Scientific Advertising, C. Hopkins (MacGibbon and Key, 1968)
* Television Advertising, D. Ingman (Business Publications, 1965)

Advertising Research
  Assessing the Effectiveness of Advertising, M. Lovell and J. Potter (Business Books, 1975)
* Measuring Advertising, Readership and Results, D. Starch (McGraw Hill, 1966)
  Testing to Destruction, A. Hedges (IPA)

Sales Promotion
* Marketing Below-the-Line, M. Christopher (Allen and Unwin, 1972)
* Sales Promotion (Second Edition), P. Spillard (Business Books)

Printing and Reproduction
* Printing Reproduction Pocket Pal (Advertising Agency Production Association, 1976)
* Processes of Graphic Reproduction in Printing, H. Curwen (Faber & Faber, 1967)

Law and Controls
* Advertising Law Handbook (Second Edition), D. Woolley (Business Books, 1976)
* British Code of Advertising Practice, (Advertising Standards Authority)
* The Consumer, Society and the Law, Borrie & Diamond (Penguin, 1966)

Victorian Advertisements, L. de Vries (John Murray, 1968)

International

Advertising and Socialism, P. Hanson (Advertising Association, 1974)

Advertising Conditions in Various Countries, (IPA Leaflets)

* International Marketing, Miracle and Albaum (Irwin, 1970)
* Marketing Management for Europe, C. S. Deverell (Butterworth, 1969)

Careers

A Career in an Advertising Agency, (IPA)

150 Careers in Advertising, P. Mann (Longman, 1971)

Index

OFFICE MANAGEMENT

P. W. Betts

The role of the office manager has completely changed in recent years, but the critical part he plays in determining the success of a concern still remains often unrecognised.

The on-going business is dependent upon successful administrative operations at all organisation levels. Hence the generation of more and more paperwork and the ever increasing demand for administrative staff, but more paper and staff are not necessarily the answer. Increased administrative expertise is essential and the author examines here the information and techniques that are needed by the departmental office manager to be successful, and introduces the overall situation in administrative management – all of which is often not appreciated by students studying this subject or by executives who determine organisation structure.

An invaluable text for students of management studies and in particular for students of the Diploma in Administrative Management, the Certificate in Office Supervision and of the Final Examinations of the Institute of Chartered Secretaries and Administrators, the Institute of Cost and Management Accounting and the Association of Certified Accountants.

Readers in USA, please write to
David McKay Company, Inc., 2 Park Avenue,
New York, NY 10016

TEACH YOURSELF BOOKS

OPERATIONAL RESEARCH

M. S. Makower and E. Williamson

Operational Research is the application of scientific method to management decision-making. It is being used to tackle a wide variety of problems, ranging from space-exploration to the control of supermarket stocks.

This book introduces and discusses some of the more important techniques which have been developed to help solve such problems. These include forecasting methods, the theory of queues, linear programming, and network analysis. Explanation and illustration of these techniques is carried out through worked examples, and each chapter ends with further exercises (and solutions) to enable the reader to test his understanding of the methods described.

Operational Research is a fascinating and increasingly topical subject. Those with a slight taste for numbers and at least some recollection of school mathematics should follow with ease the ideas presented.

An introduction to OR for business and management students and for all those involved in forecasting, planning, and decision-making.

Readers in USA, please write to
David McKay Company, Inc., 2 Park Avenue,
New York, NY 10016

TEACH YOURSELF BOOKS

ORGANISATION AND METHODS

R. G. Breadmore

Organisation and methods (O & M) can be defined as the systematic application of common sense to business problems. O & M techniques enable work to be simplified and more efficiently organised, and thus work time to be better allocated.

This book explains what O & M is, what it sets out to do and why, and illustrates how it can be applied in practice to most common business functions. It is based upon extensive practical experience and gives a down-to-earth, step-by-step guide to enable anyone concerned with office routines to apply the techniques to their work.

Readers in USA, please write to
David McKay Company, Inc., 2 Park Avenue,
New York, NY 10016

TEACH YOURSELF BOOKS

TEACH YOURSELF BOOKS